A Chronicle of Earth in Deep Time

© 2018 Edward J. Williams and Patrick B. Williams

All rights reserved. No part of this book may be reproduced or transmitted without permission.

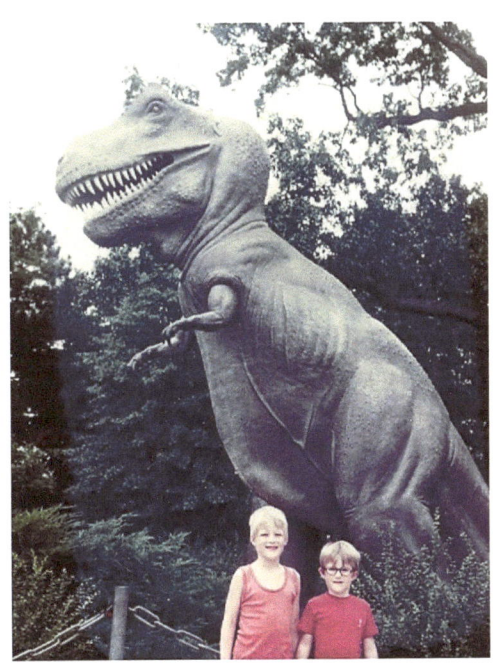

Dedicated to Mom and Dad

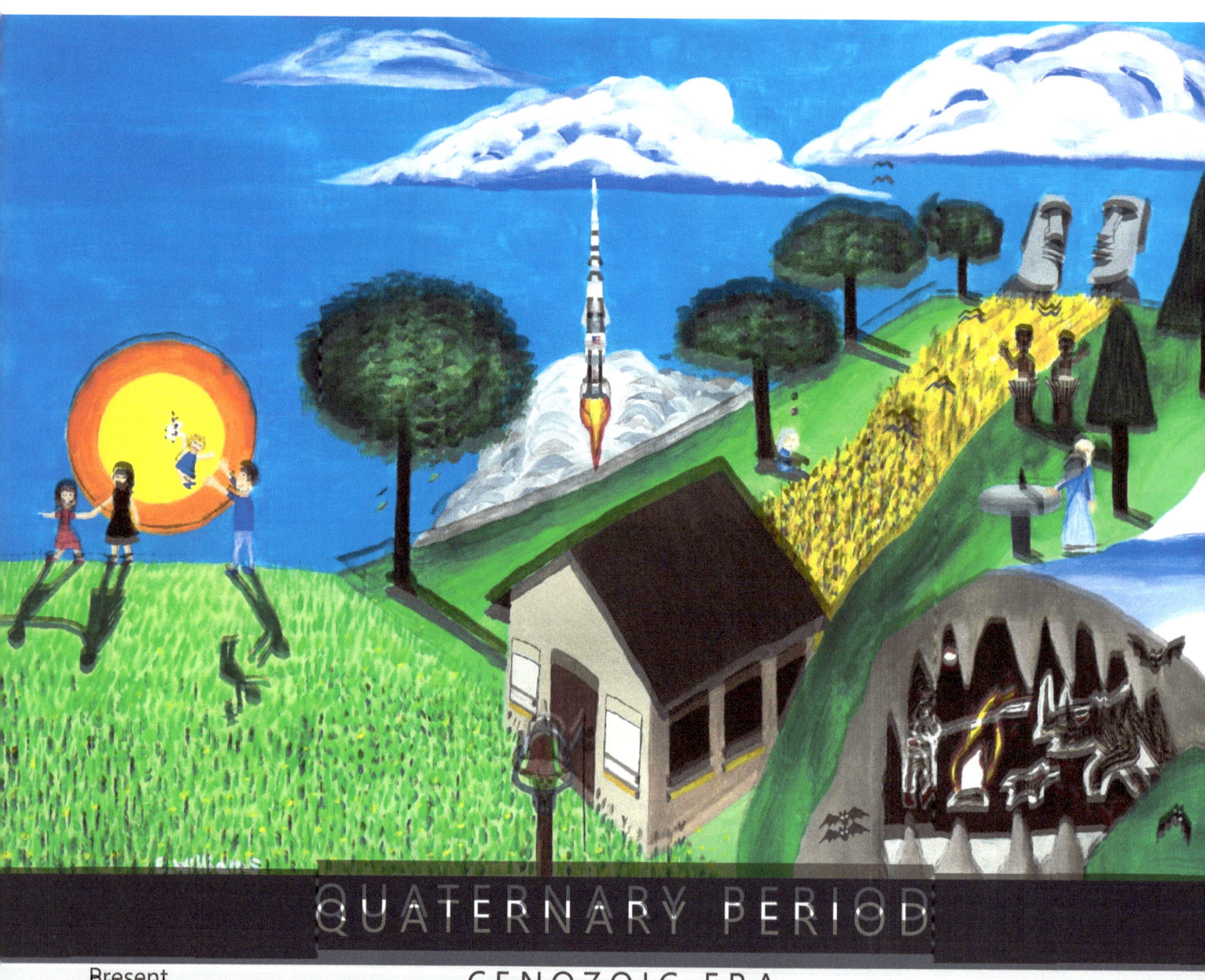

QUATERNARY PERIOD

Present
PHANEROZOIC EON
CENOZOIC ERA

"The Best of All Worlds"

Modern *Homo sapiens* dwells on Earth aesthetically. Art, music, agriculture, history, philosophy, education, science, and engineering, are developed by humans. Humans travel to the Moon. Humans develop a sense of free play – a circular time that transcends the linear time of the rest of the mural – allowing them to imagine counterfactual situations. The child leads her parents smiling into an unknown future, knowing it is infinite with possibility...

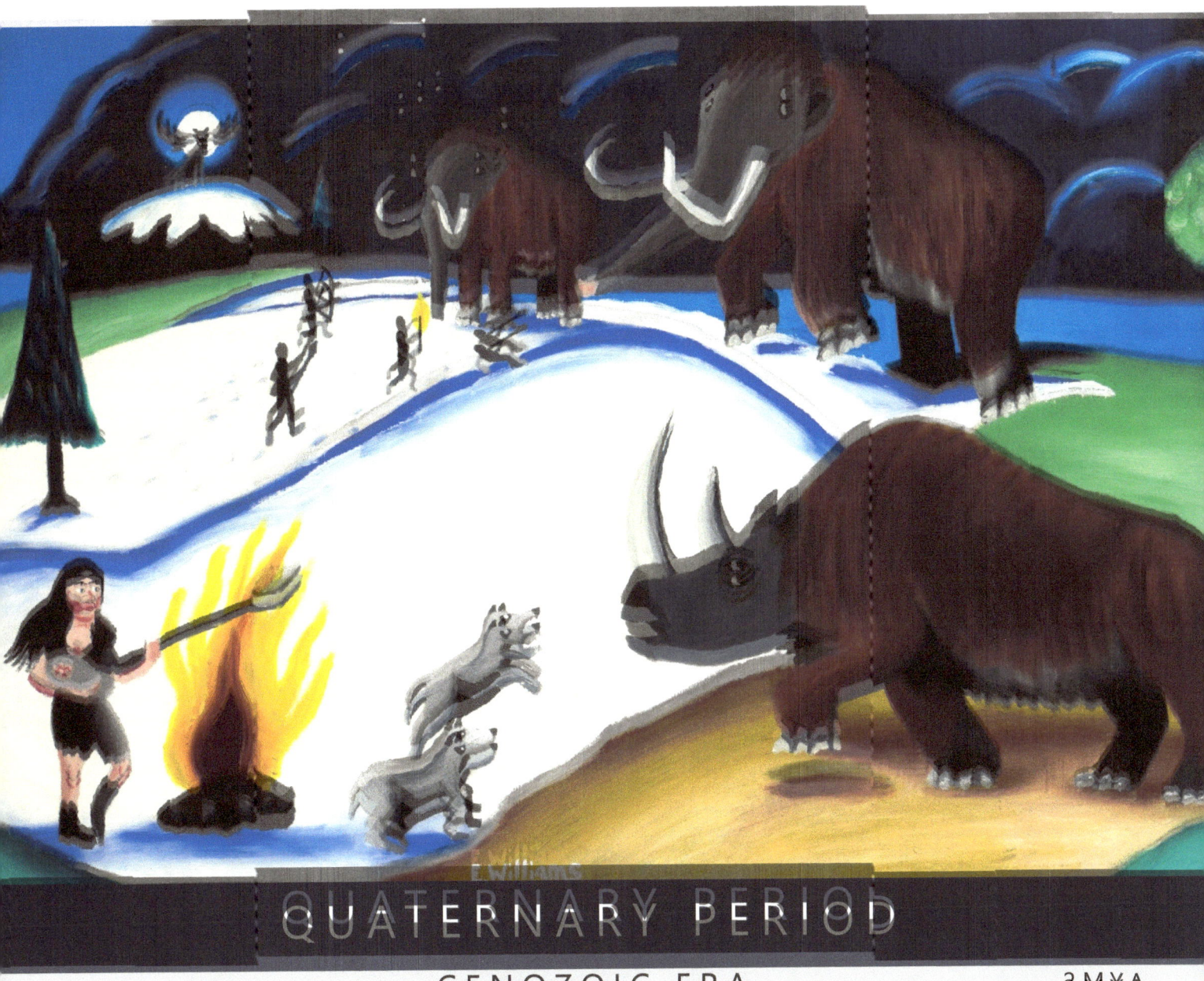

QUATERNARY PERIOD
CENOZOIC ERA — 2 M.Y.A.

"Man's Best Friend"

A tribe of *Homo neanderthalensis* hunts the Woolly Mammoth *Mammuthus primigenius* during the Ice Age. Newly domesticated wolves *Canis lupus* defend a young woman and her baby from a Woolly Rhinoceros *Coelodonta antiquitatis*. Humans have developed more sophisticated weapons and the use of fire. In the moonlight, the giant Irish Elk *Megaloceros giganteus* looks on.

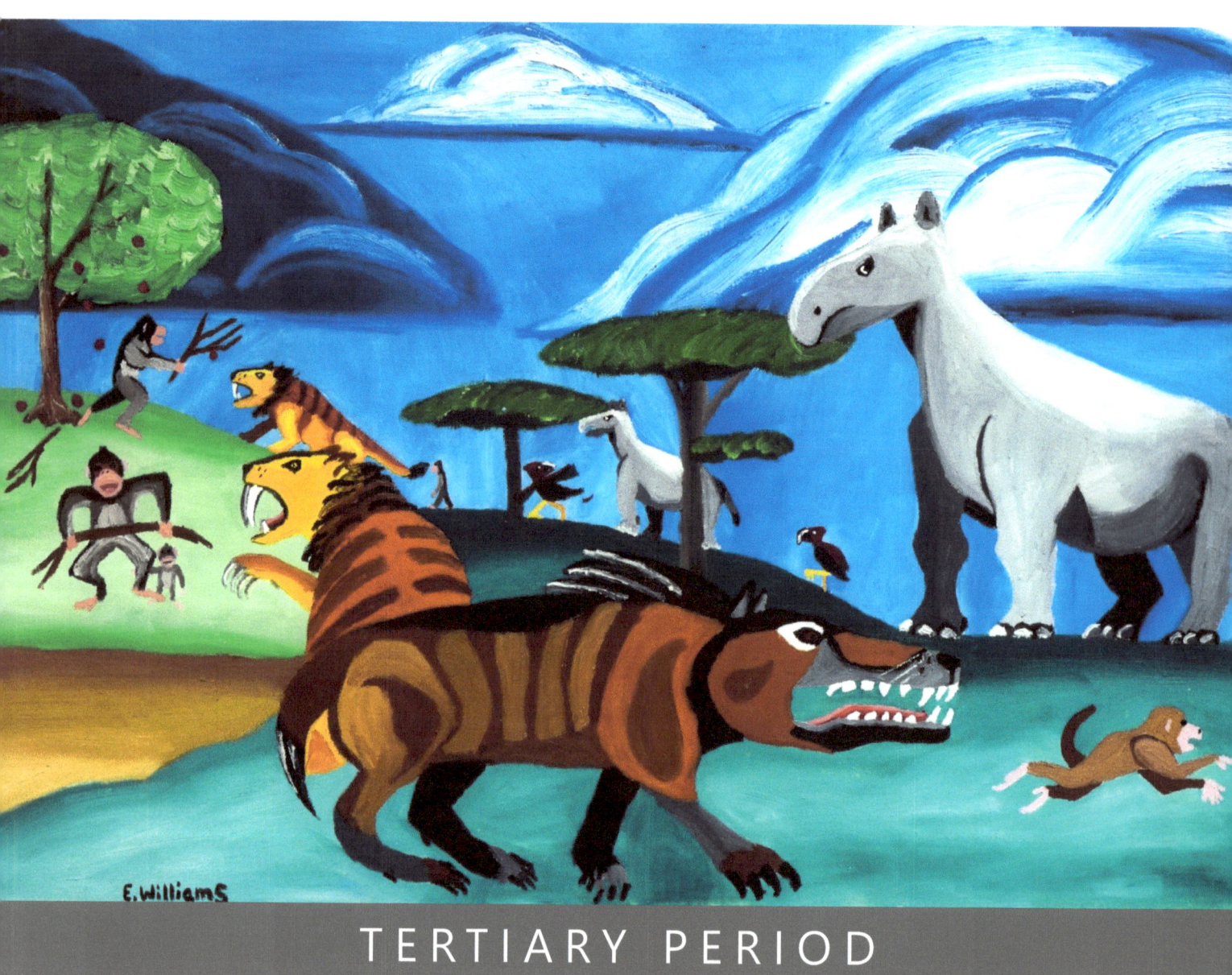

TERTIARY PERIOD

2 M.Y.A.
PHANEROZOIC EON

CENOZOIC ERA

"The Prey's Revenge"

Hominids evolve and begin to show startling displays of abstract thinking. *Australopithecus afarensis* uses primitive weaponry made from a fruit tree against the Sabre-Tooth Tiger *Smilodon fatalis*. The largest carnivorous mammal on land is not even in the Order Carnivora: *Andrewsarchus mongoliensis*, a distant cousin to both pigs and whales, chases the monkey *Mesopithecus pentelici*. The ancestor of the rhinoceros *Indricotherium bugtiense* has become the largest terrestrial mammal ever and is no longer threatened by the Terror-Bird *Phorusrhacos longissimus*. The reign of the Archosaurs is over, and the Age of Mammals truly begins.

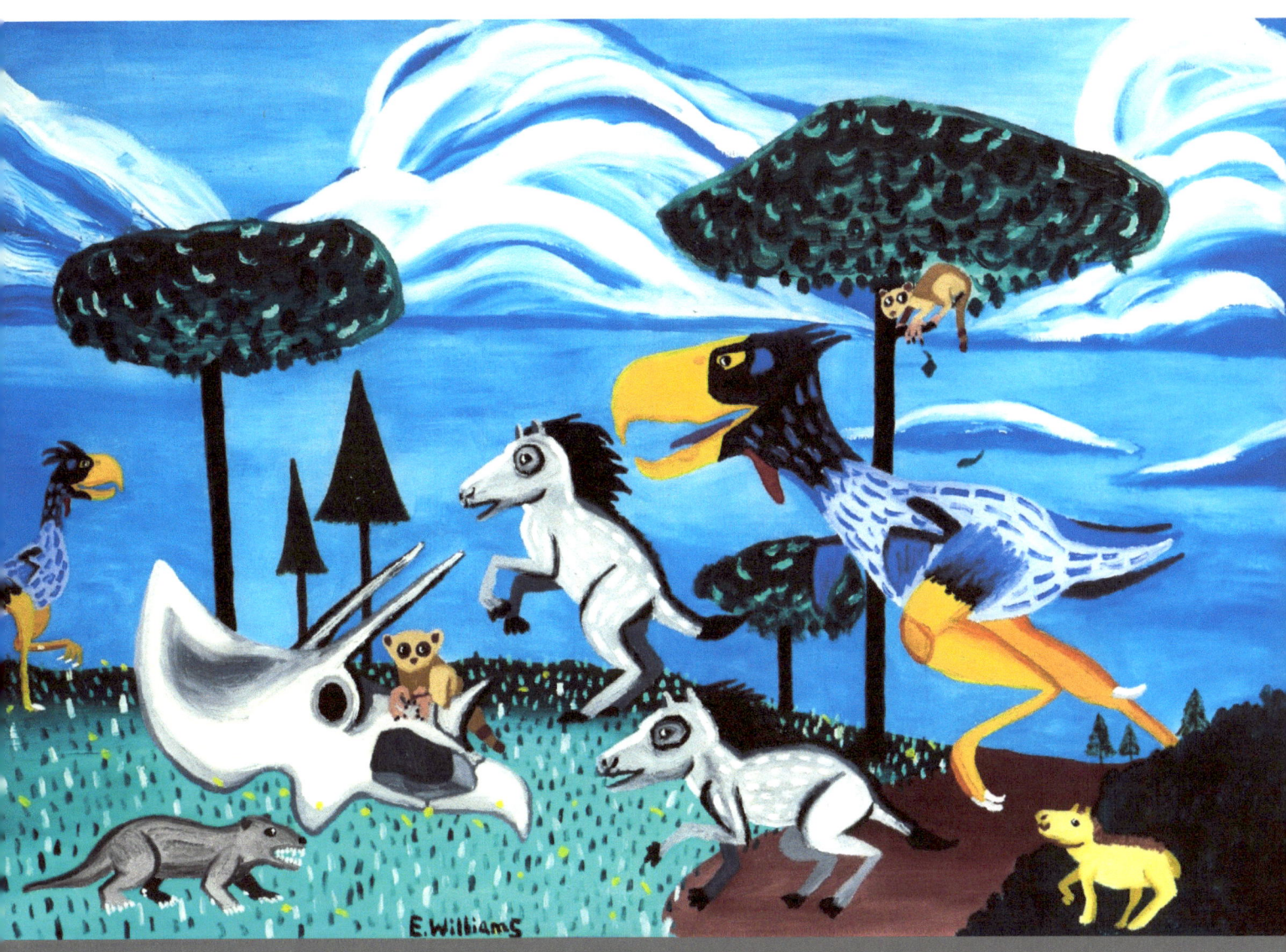

TERTIARY PERIOD

CENOZOIC ERA

65 M.Y.A.

"Inheritors"

The comet has hit and the Age of Dinosaurs has ended. Primates evolve, and the prosimian *Necrolemur antiquus* sits on the skull of *Triceratops horridus*. But the reign of the Archosaurs is not quite over. The Terror-Bird *Diatryma gigantea* hunts the ancestral horse *Mesohippus bairdi* as the even more primitive horse *Eohippus angustidens* looks on. *Mesohippus* is also startled by an ancestor of the carnivores, *Miacis parvivorus*. Grass now grows on the Earth, along with Maple and Oak trees.

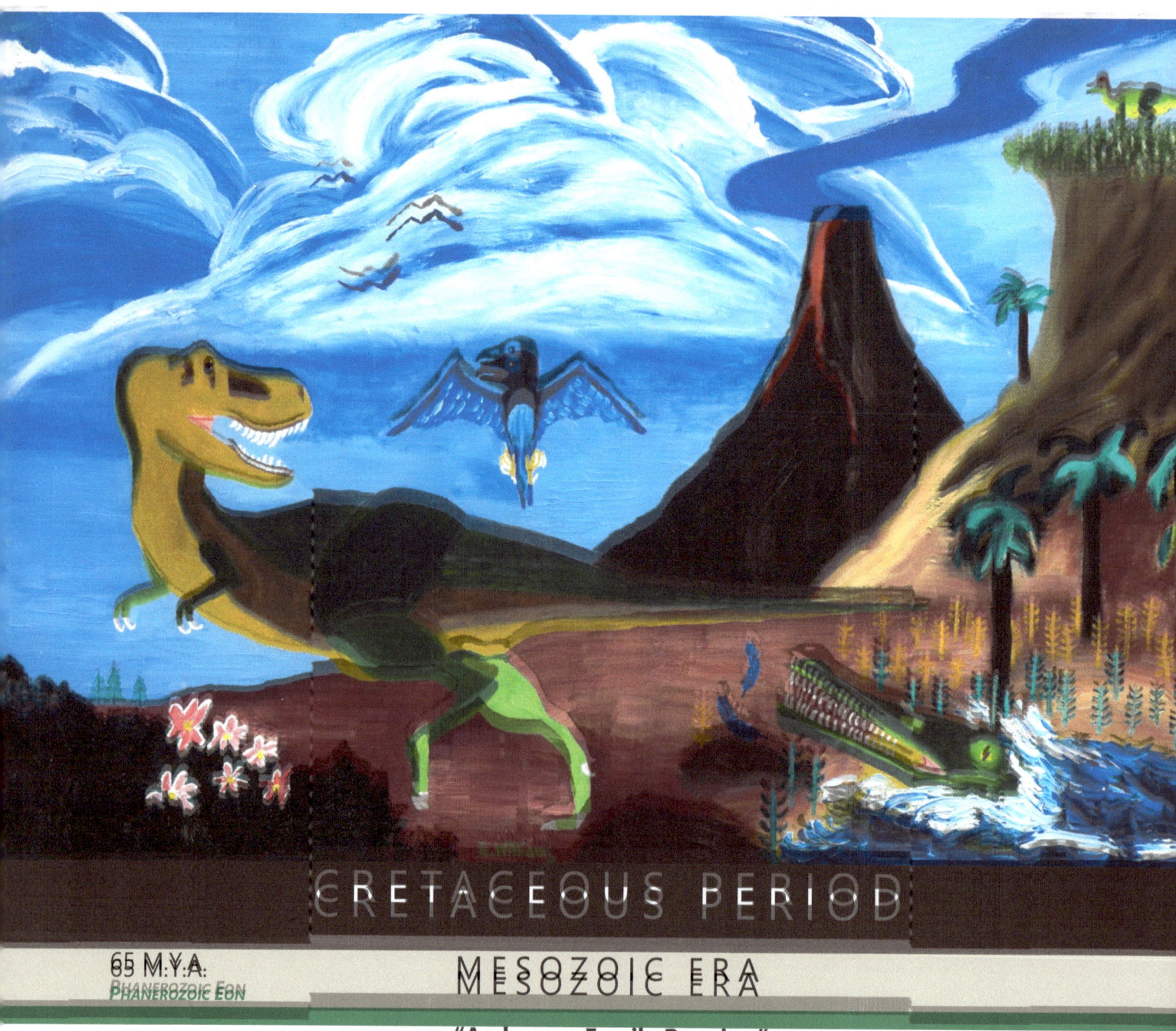

"Archosaur Family Reunion"

The king of the tyrant lizards *Tyrannosaurus rex* is startled by the immense crocodile *Deinosuchus rugosus* chasing a bird. All three can be considered examples of diapsid Archosaurs, but only two will survive the collision about to occur. Flowers become abundant on Earth, beginning the dominance of Angiosperms on the planet. *Corythosaurus casuarius* observes the action.

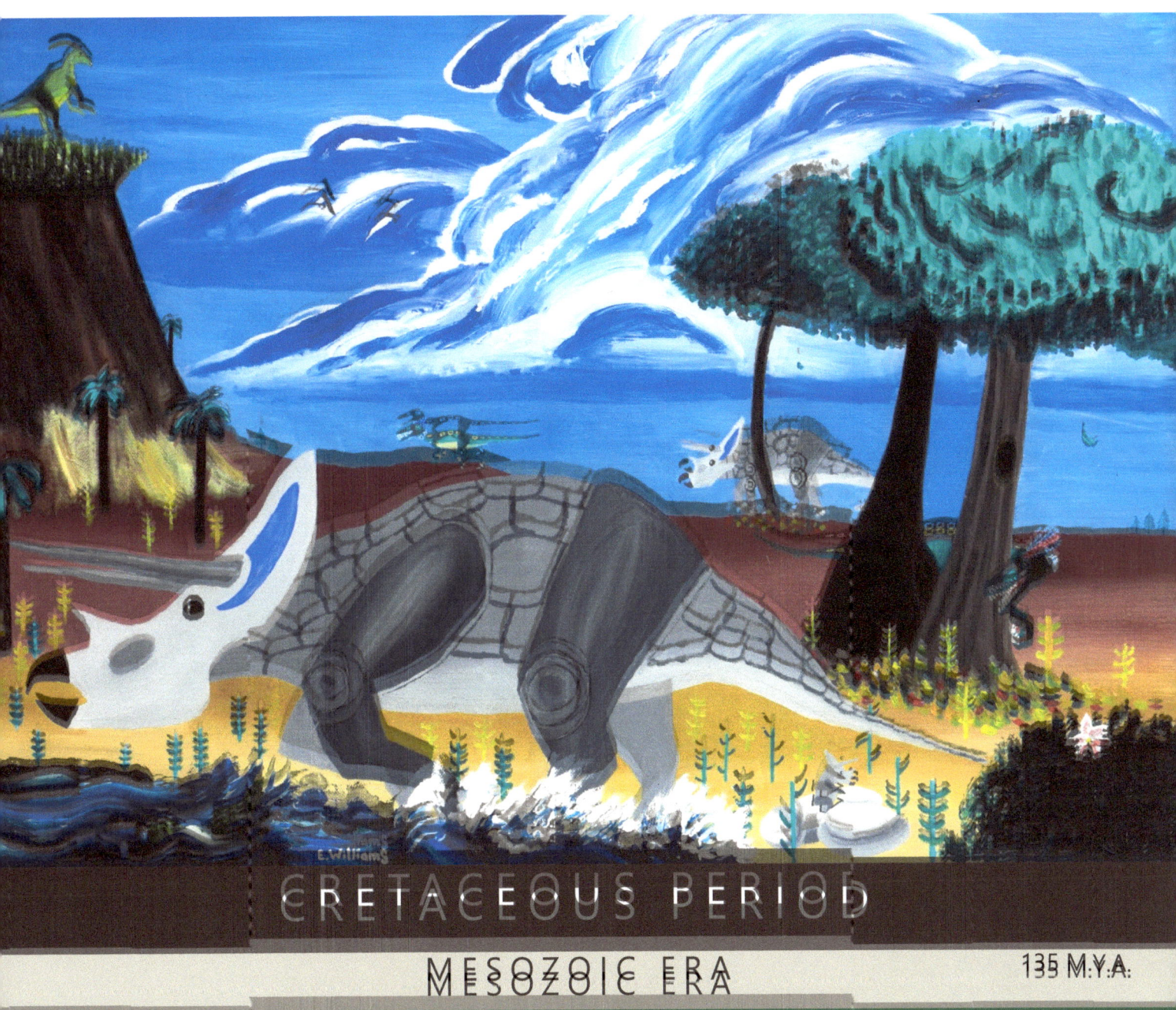

"Three-Horned Face"

Triceratops horridus defends her babies from marauding *Deinonychus antirrhopus*, frightening the prehistoric crocodile *Deinosuchus rugosus*. *Parasaurolophus walkeri* looks on in the distance, as *Pteranodon longiceps* dominates the sky. Palm trees evolve.

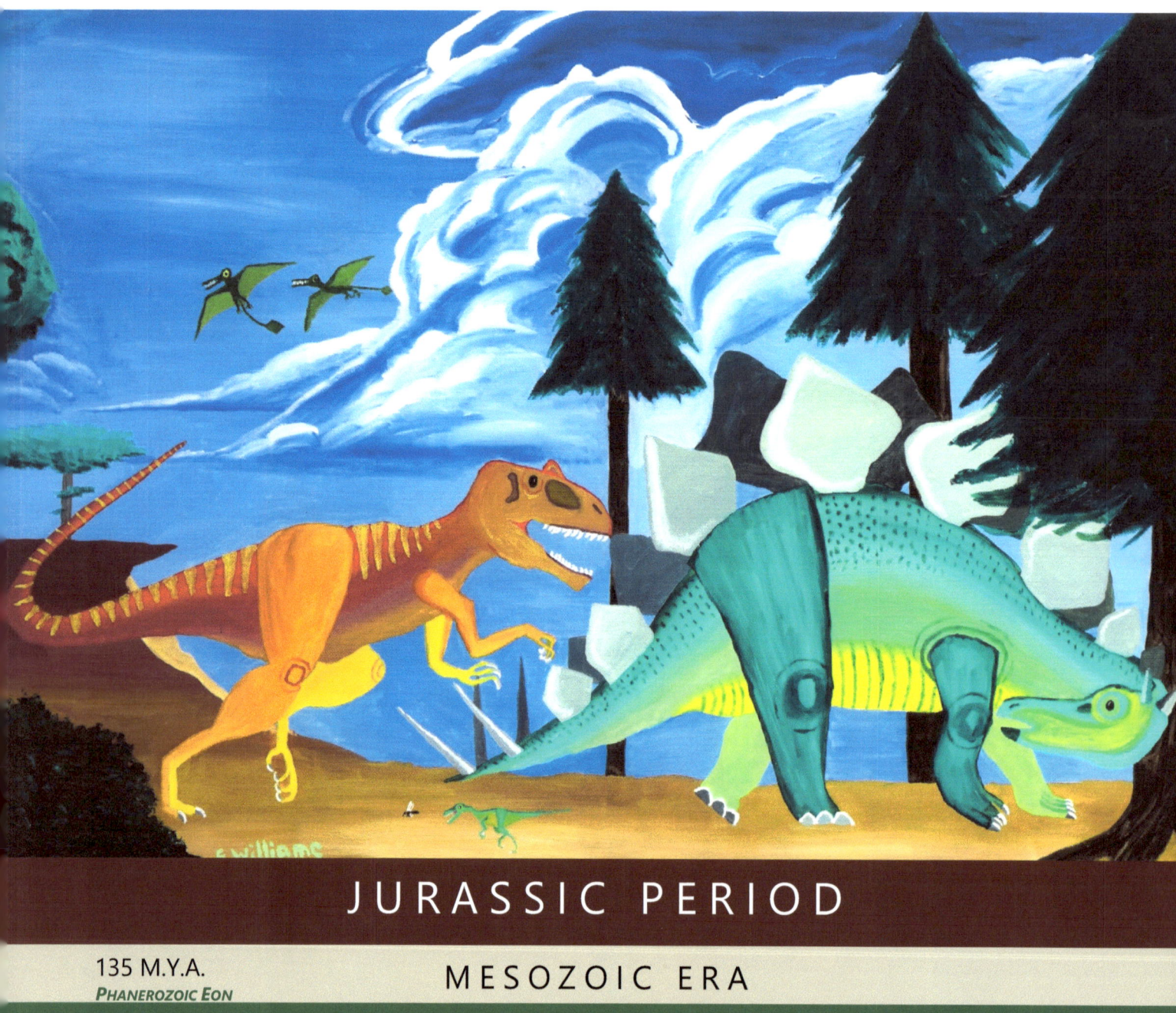

JURASSIC PERIOD

135 M.Y.A.
PHANEROZOIC EON

MESOZOIC ERA

"Tiger of the Jurassic"

The fearsome *Allosaurus atrox* prepares to attack a well-defended *Stegosaurus stenops*. In the foreground, the tiny Dinosaur *Compsognathus longipes* hunts an insect, while *Rhamphorhynchus longicaudus* flies freely in the sky. Pangea begins to break up and Sassafras trees grow.

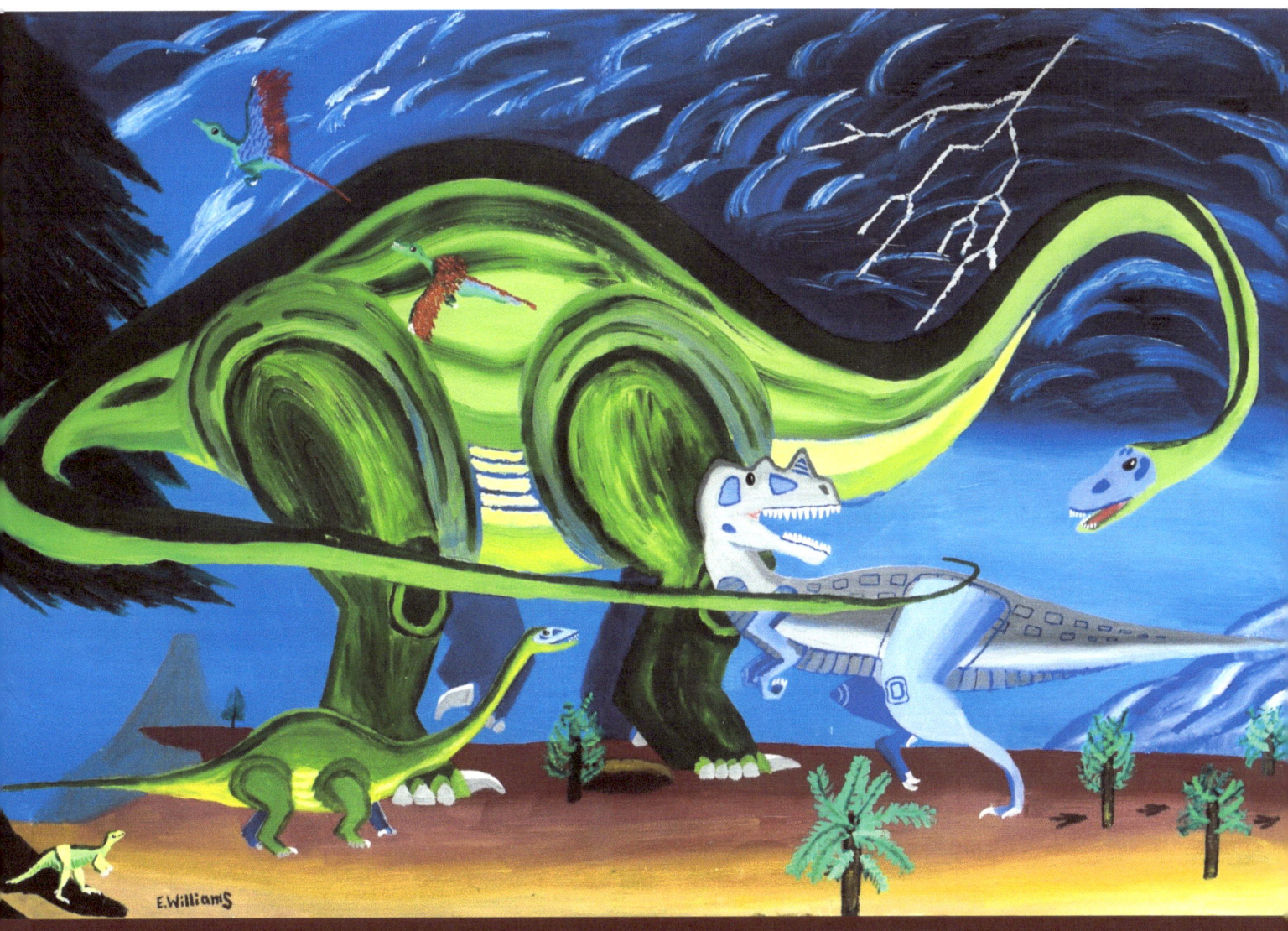

JURASSIC PERIOD

MESOZOIC ERA

200 M.Y.A.

"Thunder Lizard"

The thunder lizard *Brontosaurus excelsus* defends her baby against an extremely unwise *Ceratosaurus nasicornis*. The feathered *Archaepoteryx lithographica* takes flight as lightning strikes. The first Ornithischian (bird-hipped) Dinosaur *Lesothosaurus diagnosticus* appears in the foreground.

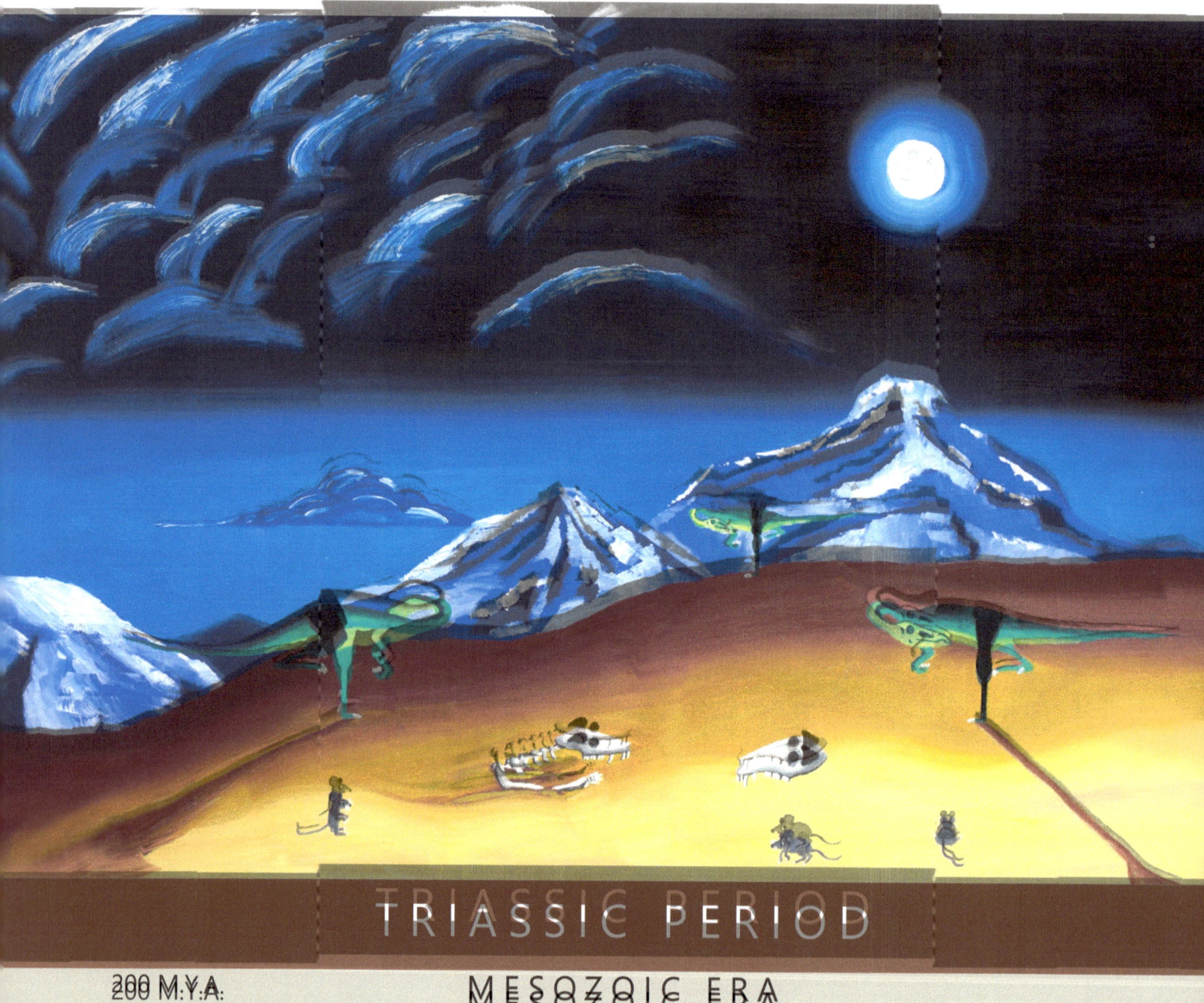

"Midnight in Pangea"

A herd of *Coelophysis bauri* sleeps flamingo-like under the moonlit sky of Pangea, the last of the supercontinents. The first mammal *Megazostrodon rudnerae*, driven from the daylight into a nocturnal existence, observes them. They are descendants of the Therapsids and Pelycosaurs, and the predecessors of all Mammals to come. Synapsid remains are visible from the Dinosaur purge.

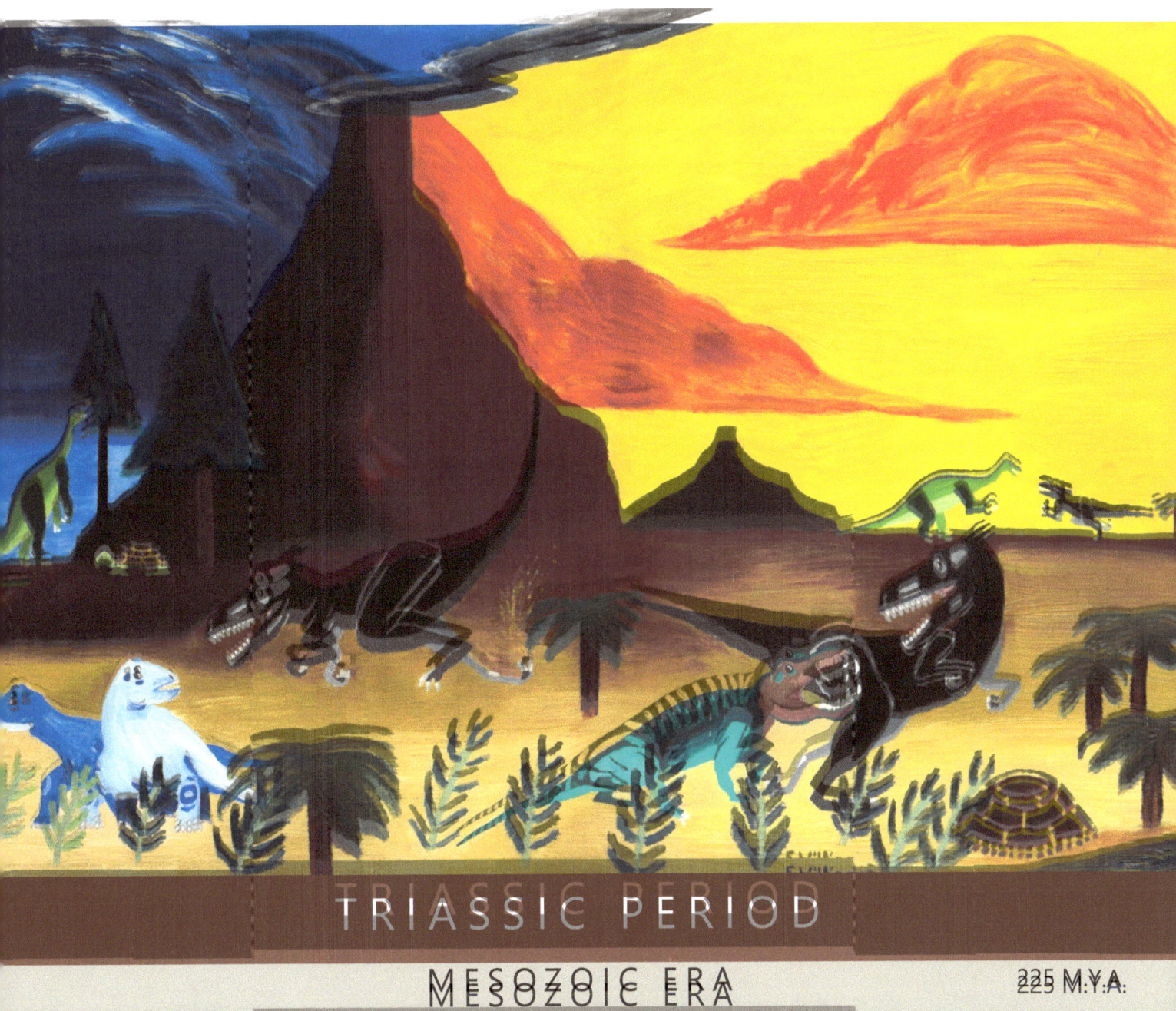

"Dawn of the Dinosaurs"

Dinosaurs walk the Earth: The bipedal nature of the Dinosaur *Herrerosaurus ischigualastensis* allows it to hunt from above the crawling Therapsids *Inostrancevia alexandri* and *Moschops capensis*, decimating them in a manner that will not be matched until the appearance of Man. *Plateosaurus engelhardti*, ancestral to the sauropod Dinosaurs, rears up to defend itself. Some Anapsids develop shells, evolving into the first turtle *Proganochelys quenstedti*.

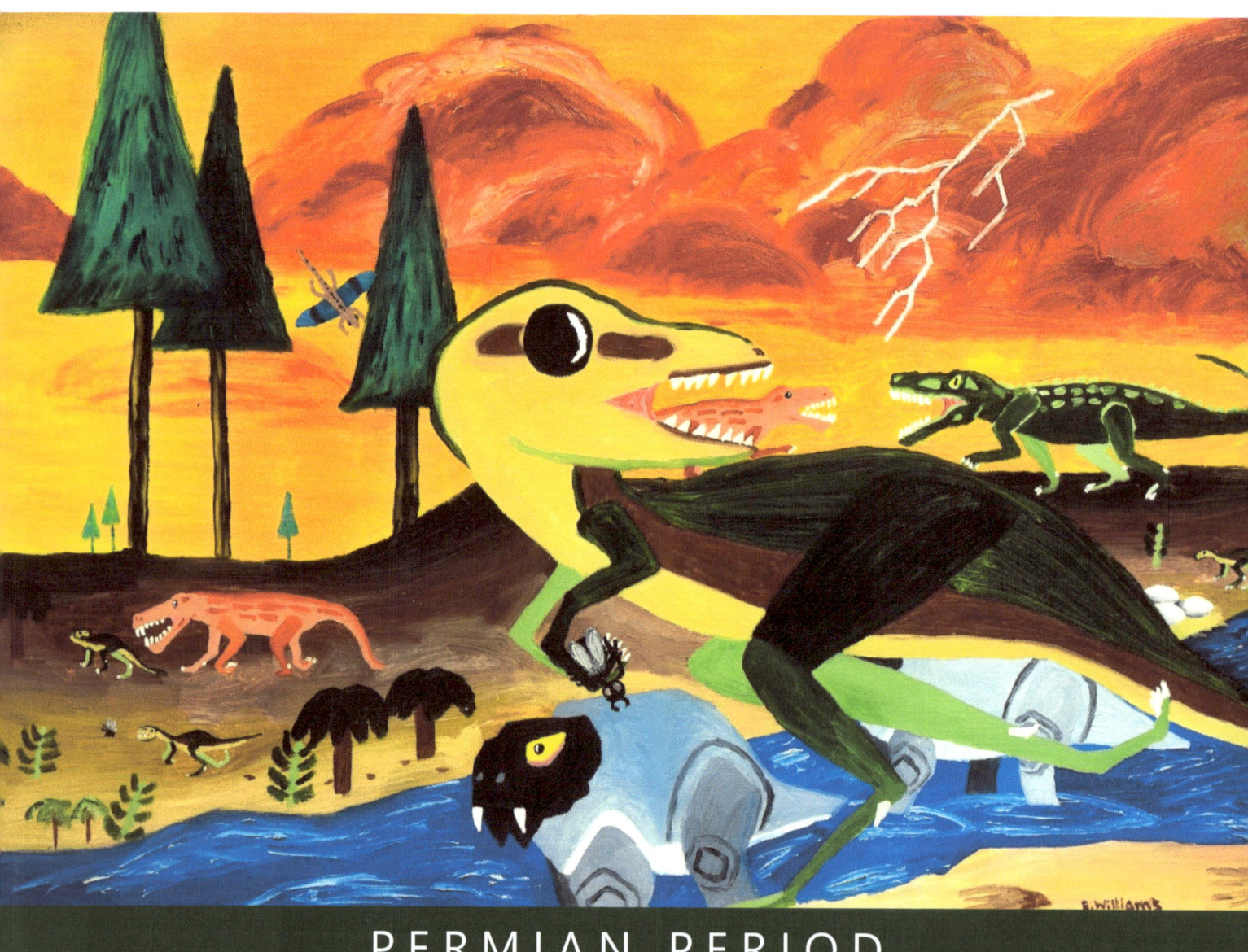

PERMIAN PERIOD

225 M.Y.A.
PHANEROZOIC EON

PALEOZOIC ERA

"Thecodont"

Diapsid reptiles, distinguished by two openings in their skull behind the orbit, evolve. Synapsid Therapsids (mammal-like reptiles) evolve from Pelycosaurs and will eventually give rise to all mammals. The diapsid Thecodont *Lagosuchus talampayensis* captures an insect but is menaced by the therapsid *Lycaenops ornatus*. This thecodont appears meek but is possibly an ancestor of the Dinosaurs. *Lycaenops ornatus* is menaced by a diapsid reptile, the Archosaur *Erythrosuchus africanus*. The diapsid *Coelurosauravus elivensis* glides in the sky, while the armored anapsid *Scutosaurus karpinskii* marches through the river. Cycads evolve and thrive.

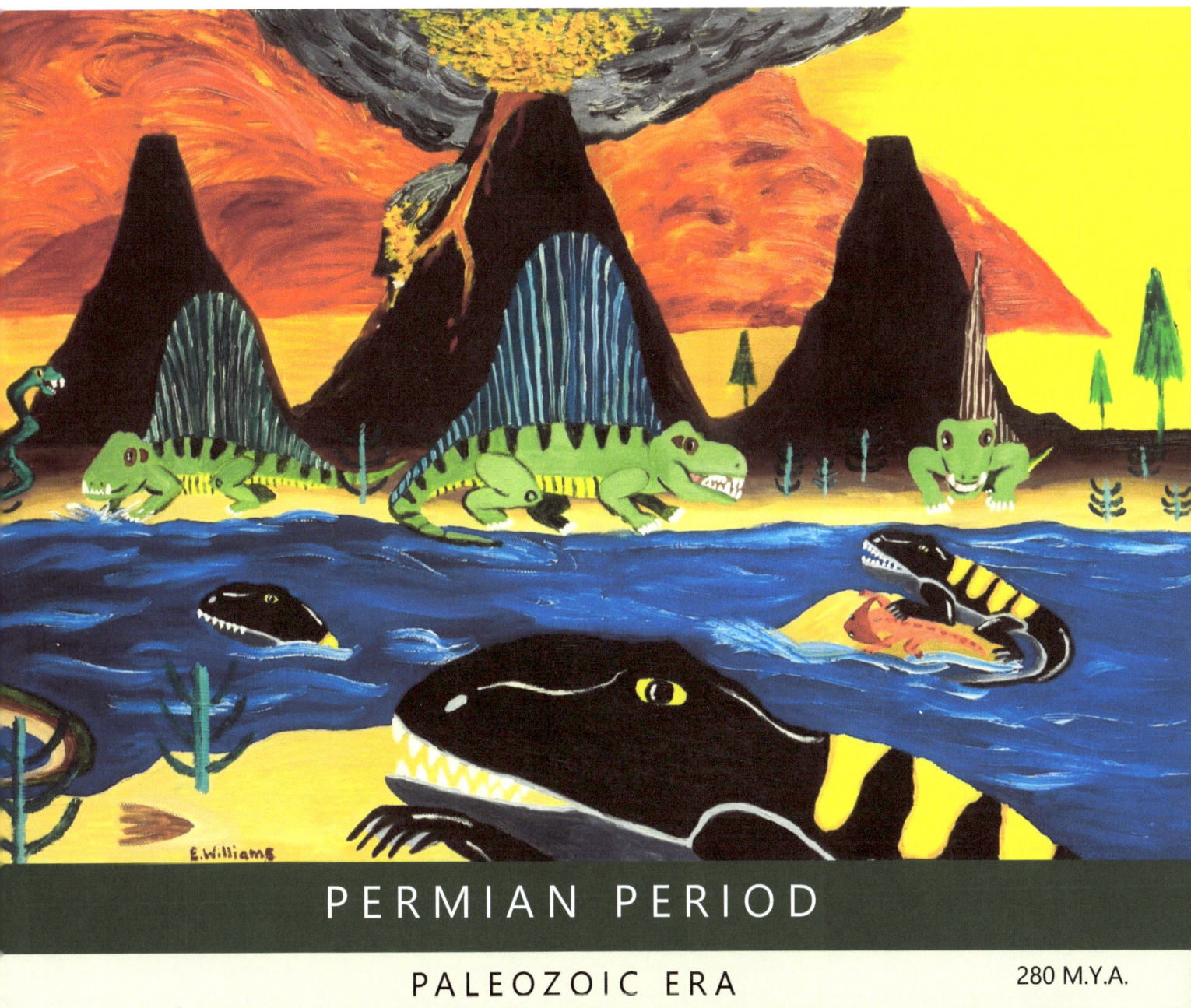

PERMIAN PERIOD

PALEOZOIC ERA   280 M.Y.A.

"Pelycosaur"

Synapsid reptiles, distinguished by a single opening in their skull behind the orbit, evolve from anapsids. The synapsid Pelycosaur *Dimetrodon limbatus* becomes the apex predator, wresting control from the amphibian *Eryops megacephalus* and the arthropods. *Eryops* still manages to prey upon the smaller, boomerang-headed amphibian *Diplocaulus salamandroides*. Snakes and Gymnosperm conifers appear and become abundant.

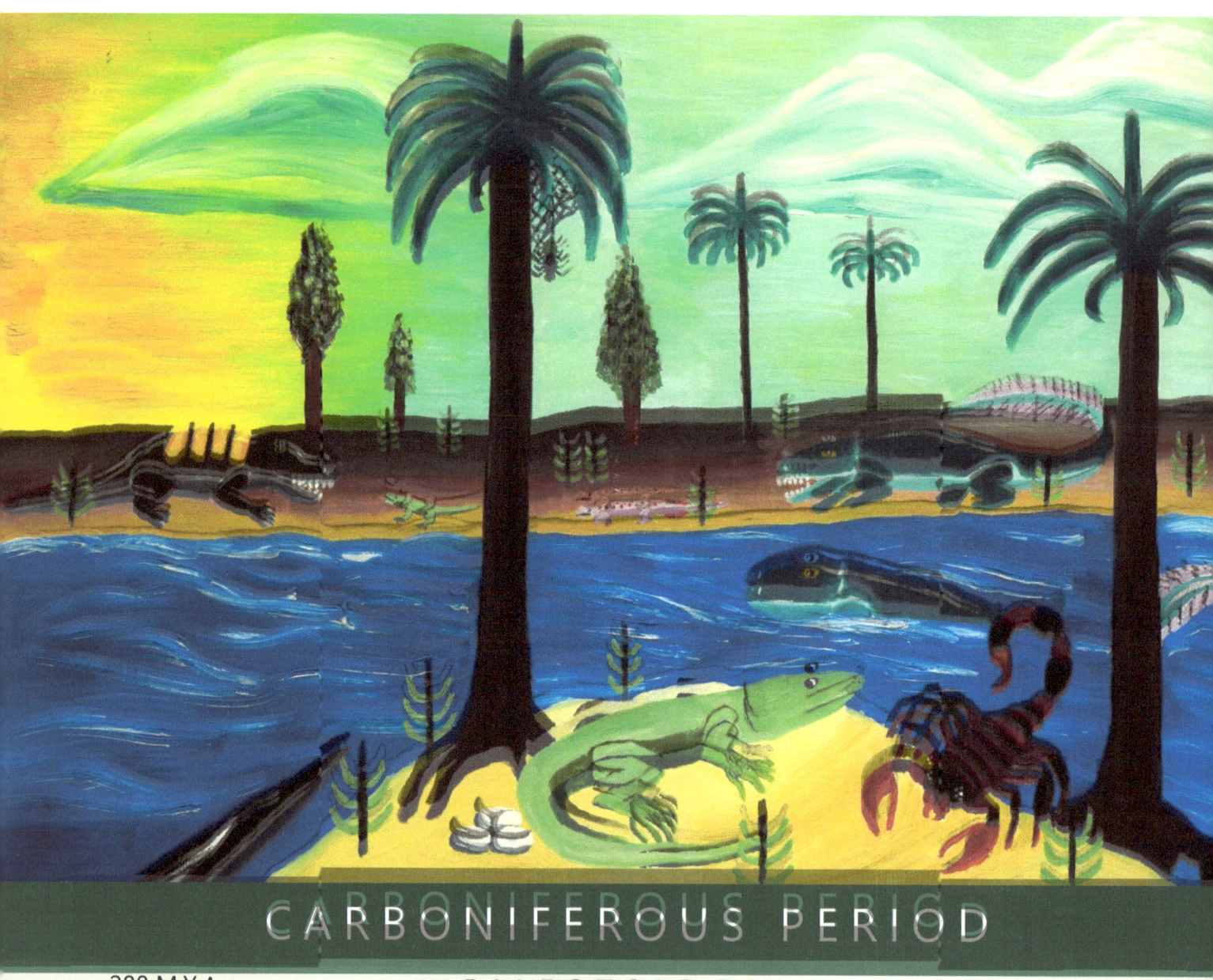

CARBONIFEROUS PERIOD

280 M.Y.A.
PALEOZOIC ERA
PHANEROZOIC EON

"Cotylosaur"

The first reptile *Hylonomus lyelli* lays its eggs on the beach, liberating itself from the sea. This is a primitive Anapsid reptile sometimes called a Cotylosaur that will give rise to several lineages: turtles (anapsids), mammals (synapsids), and birds, Dinosaurs, and alligators (diapsids). The carnivorous amphibian *Eryops megacephalus* as well as a scorpion look on menacingly. The carnivorous amphibian *Eogyrinus attheyi* preys in the water and on land on the smaller amphibian *Keraterpeton galvani*. Spiders evolve and begin spinning their webs.

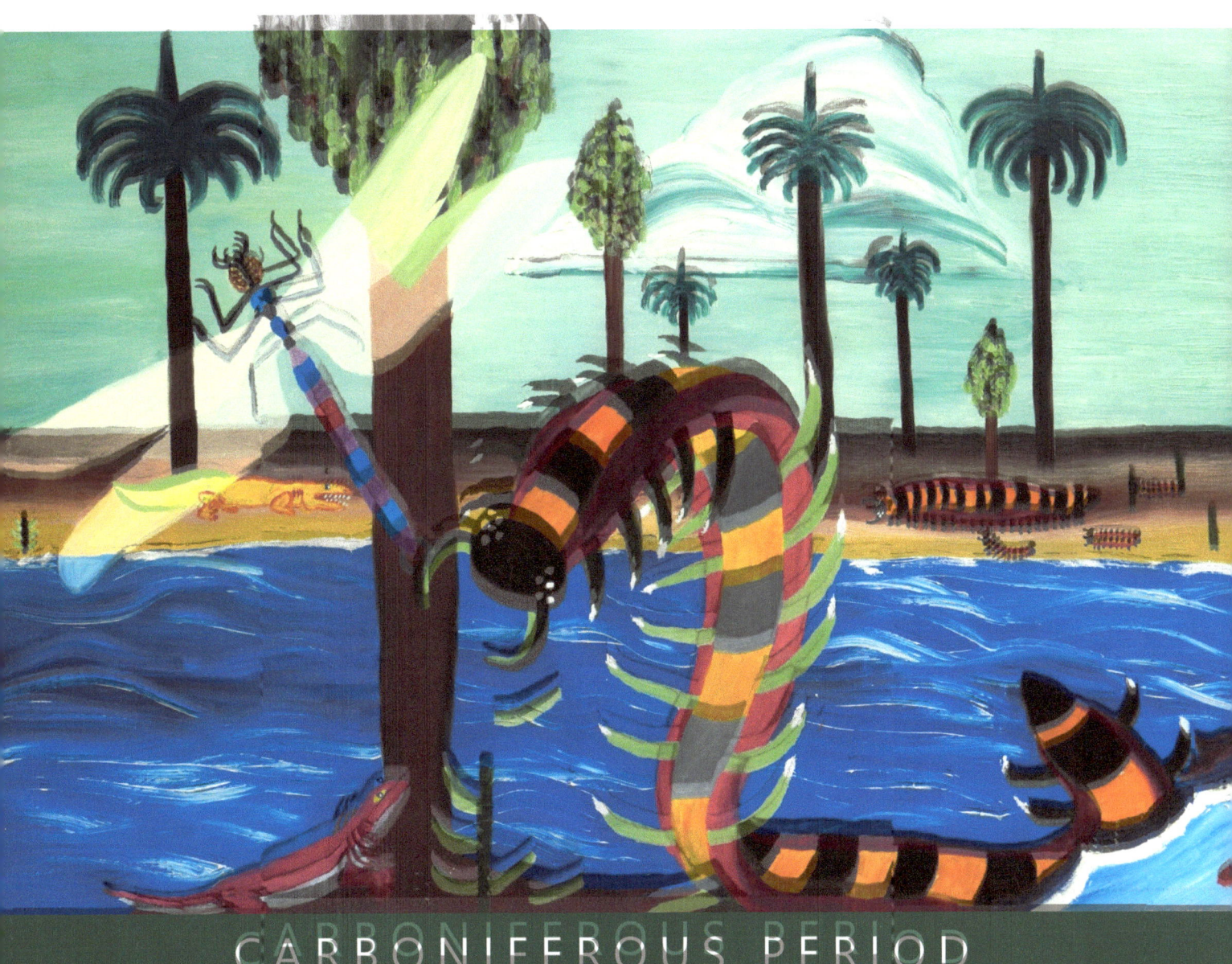

CARBONIFEROUS PERIOD
PALEOZOIC ERA
345 M.Y.A.

"Flight"

Atmospheric oxygen levels reach 35%, far higher than in today's world. This allows Arthropods to grow to massive size. The man-size millipede *Arthropleura armata* menaces the small amphibian *Microbrachis pelikani*, which retains its external gills into adulthood. A family of *Arthropleura* stalk the amphibian *Greererpeton burkemorani*. The giant insect dragonfly *Meganeura brongniarti* takes flight, as Arthropods dominate the land and air.

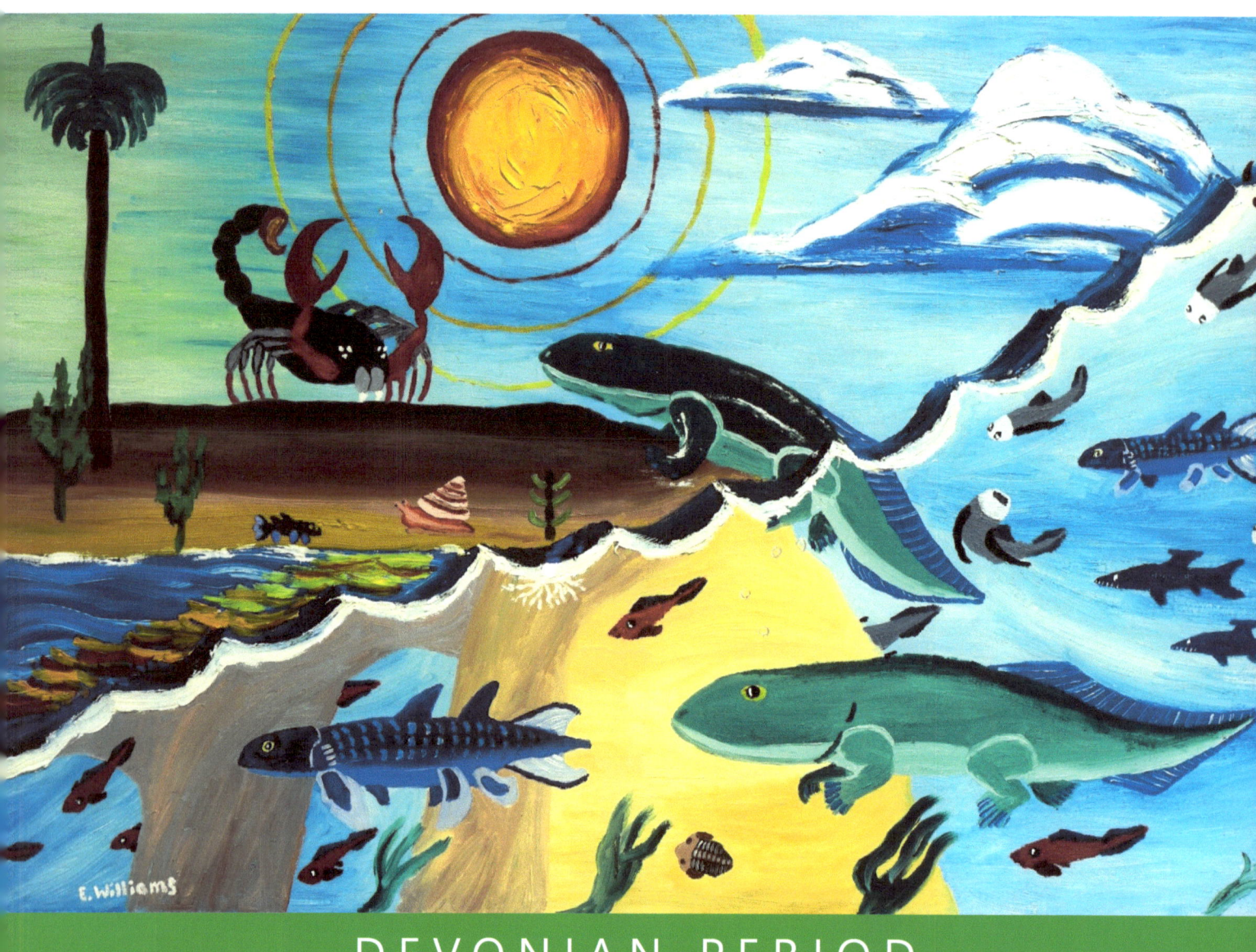

DEVONIAN PERIOD

345 M.Y.A.
PHANEROZOIC EON

PALEOZOIC ERA

"Ancient Enemies"

The first amphibian *Ichthyostega stensioei* evolves from lobe-finned fish, including *Eusthenopteron foordi*, and makes its way to land – only to find it already colonized by Arthropods. A scorpion greets it with a pose of rage. The Deuterostome Vertebrates and Protostome Arthropods remain ancient enemies on land as they were in the sea. Mollusks also colonize the land in the form of snails. Plants evolve from green algae, with tree ferns, club mosses, and horsetails thriving. The primitive shark with a brush-like fin *Stethacanthus altonensis* swims in the ocean background. We bid farewell to the Trilobites.

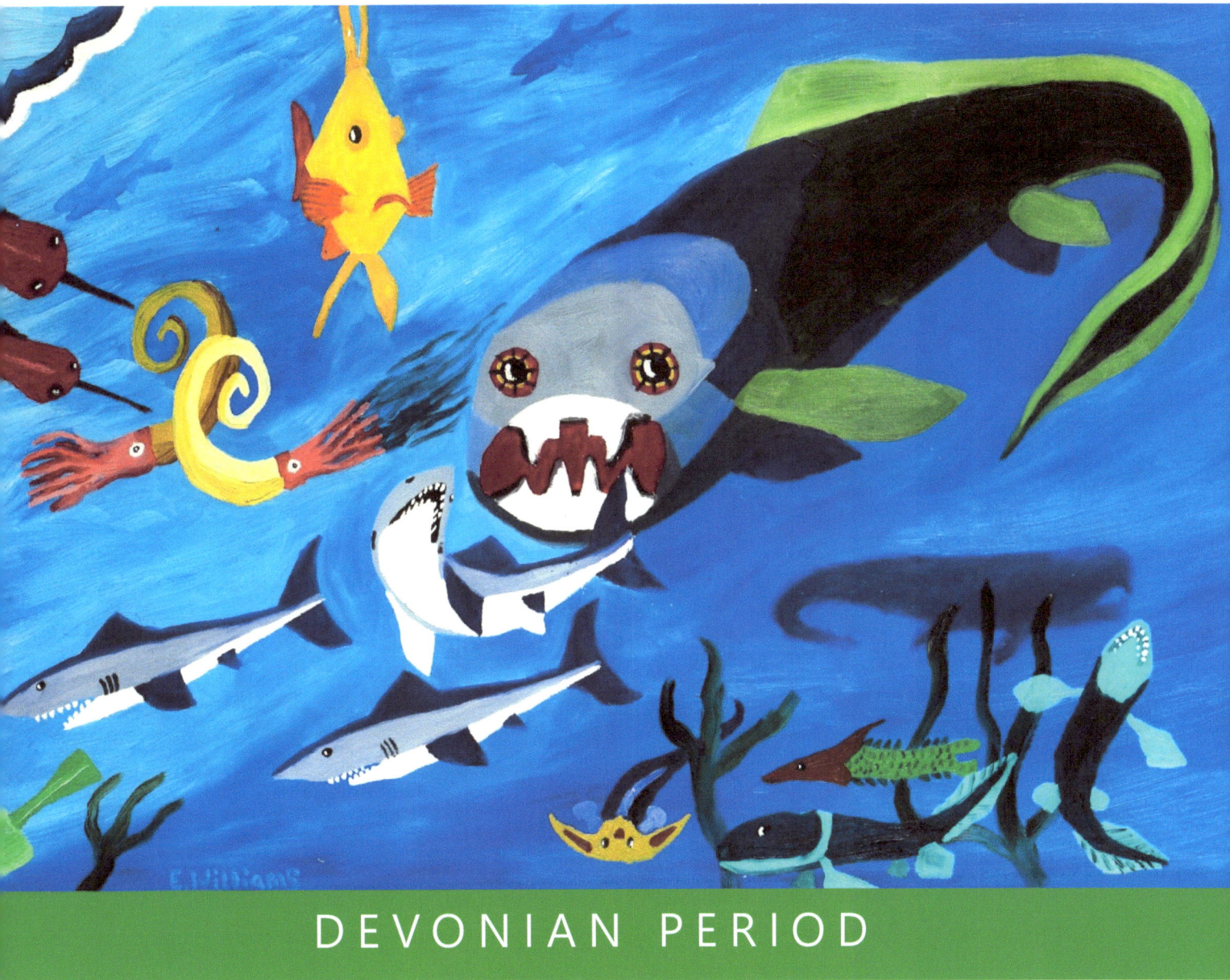

DEVONIAN PERIOD

PALEOZOIC ERA — 395 M.Y.A.

"Big Fish"

The Vertebrates gain the upper hand on the Arthropods and Mollusks. The bus-sized fish *Dunkleosteus terrella* terrorizes a group of sharks and the jawless fish *Drepanaspis gemuendenensis*. Arthropods and mollusks are no longer a match for this fish. Its teeth are actually bony projections of its massive skull. The jawless fish *Doryaspis nathorsti*, *Cephalaspis lyelli*, and *Pteraspis rostrata* keep their distance, as do a pair of lobe-finned *Tiktaalik roseae* fish.

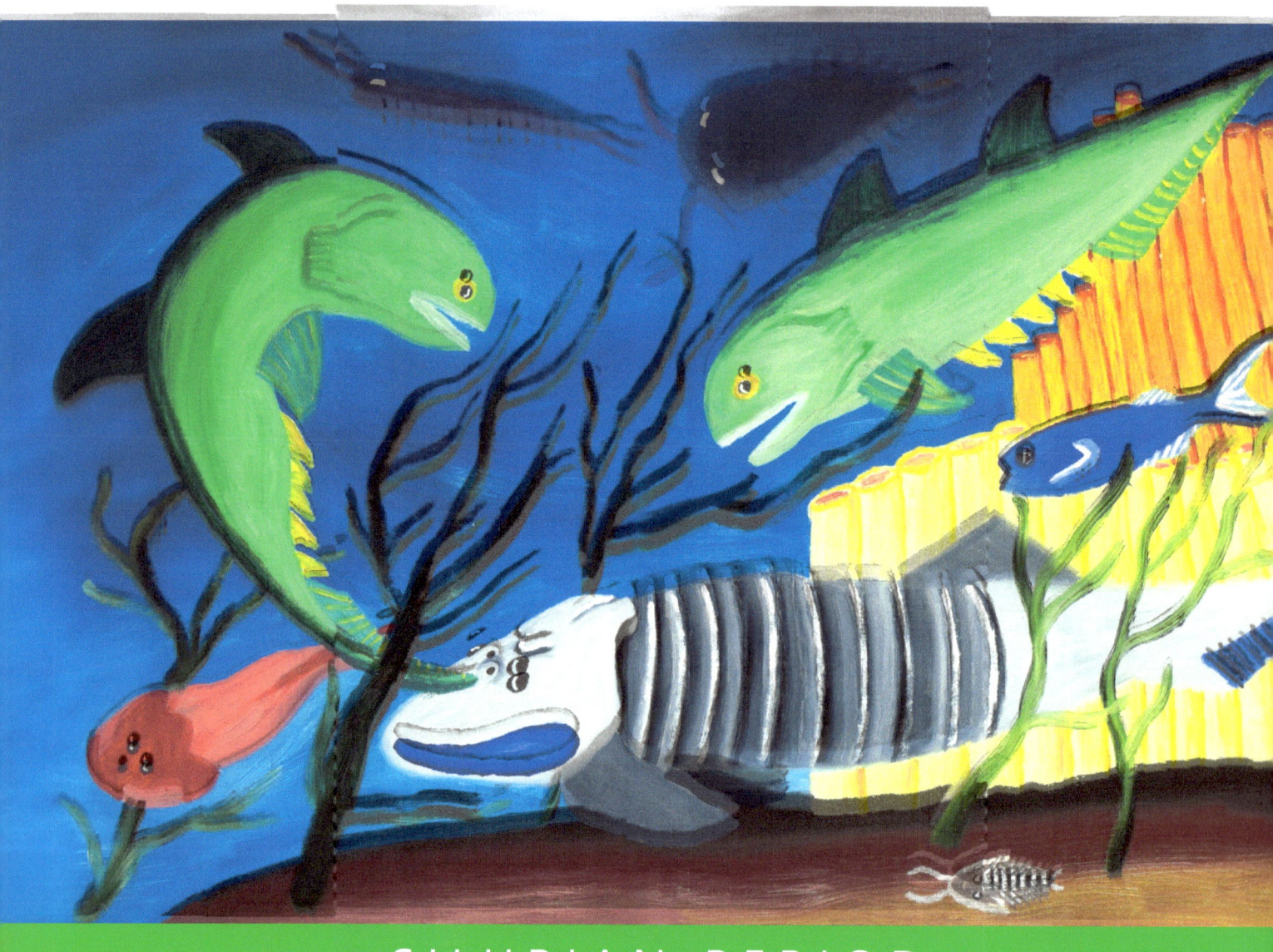

SILURIAN PERIOD

395 M.Y.A.
PALEOZOIC ERA
PHANEROZOIC EON

"Jaws"

The first jawed fish, *Climatius reticulatus*, appears, which will give rise to all jawed animals to come. The jawless fish *Hemicyclaspis murchisoni* with its head shield, along with *Thelodus parvidens* and *Dartmuthia gemmifera*, swim near the ocean bottom.

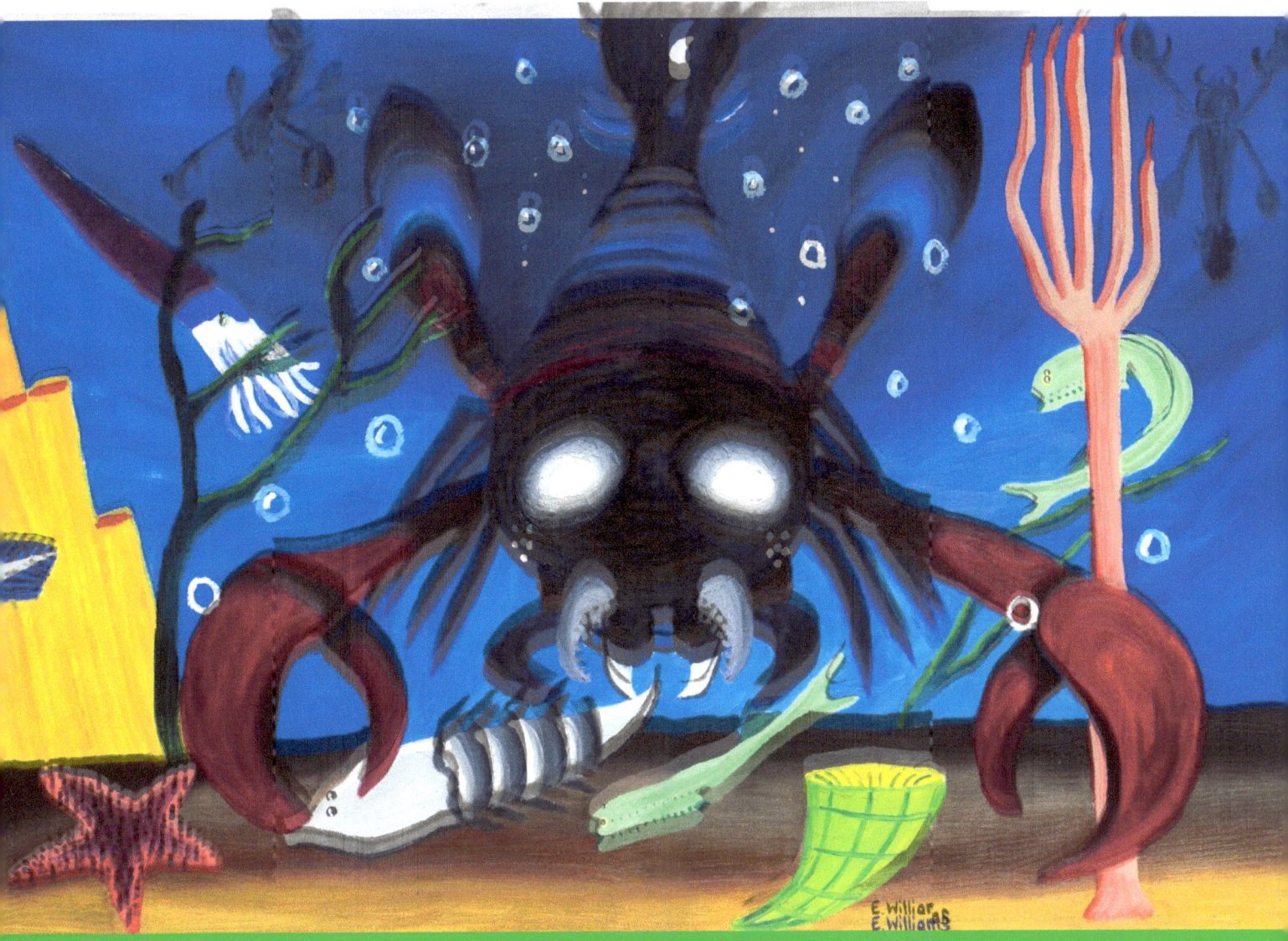

SILURIAN PERIOD

PALEOZOIC ERA 440 M.Y.A.

"Scourge of the Silurian"

The massive Arthropod sea-scorpion *Pterygotus anglicus* captures the jawless fish *Poraspis sericea* and moves in on *Jamoytius kerwoodi*. An Echinoderm starfish, a fellow Deuterostome with the vertebrates, observes this reign of Protostomes with silent pity. Horn corals and coral reefs become prevalent.

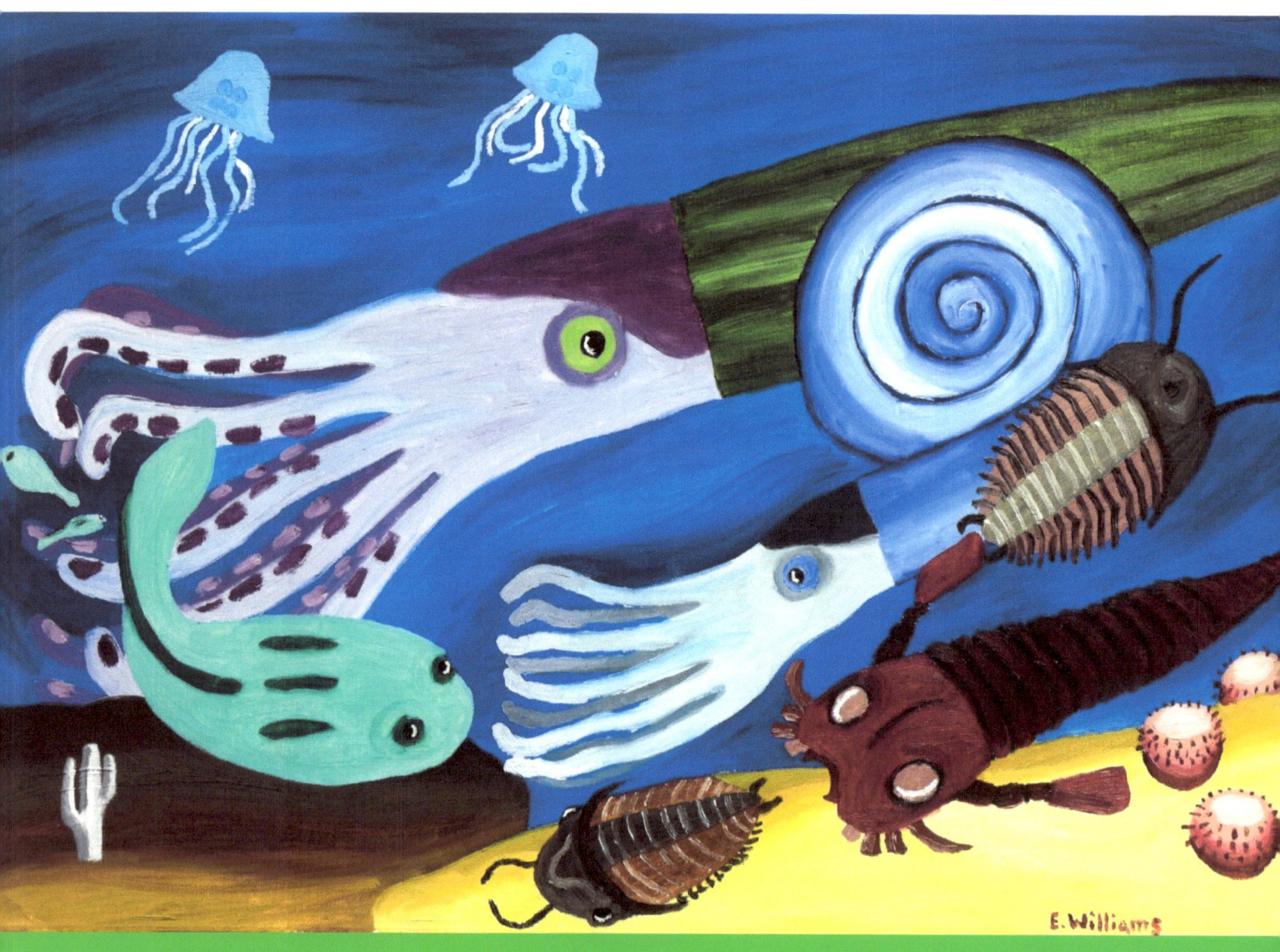

ORDOVICIAN PERIOD

440 M.Y.A.
PHANEROZOIC EON

PALEOZOIC ERA

"Sentience"

Large squids likely represent the first self-aware animals on Earth. The primitive jawless fish *Astraspis desiderata* observes them fearfully. Cnidarian Jellyfish also observe in the background. The early sea-scorpion *Pentecopterus decorahensis* menaces a Trilobite. Echinoderm sea urchins appear.

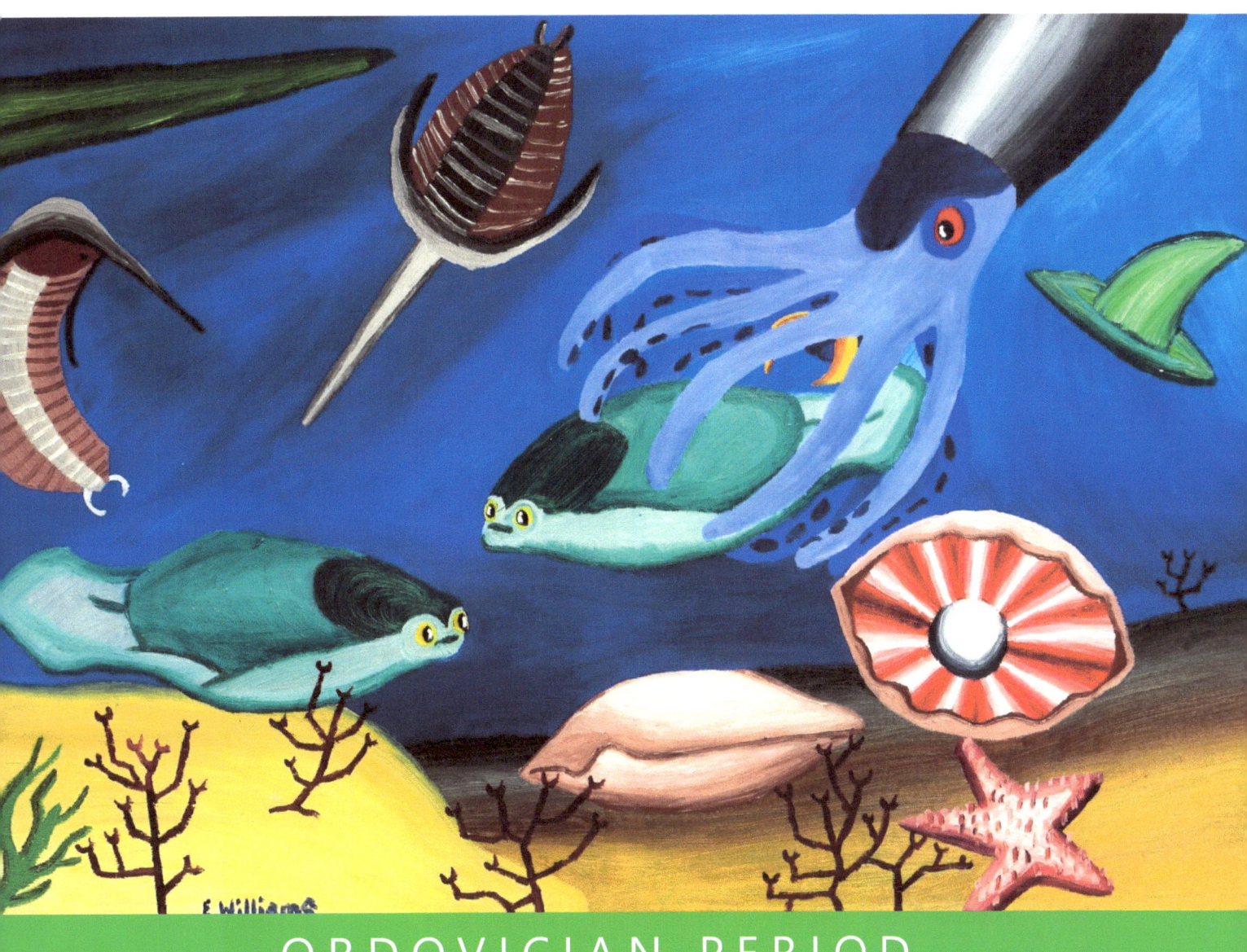

"Ascent of Mollusca"

Mollusks begin to dominate the Earth's seas. The jawless fish *Arandaspis prionotolepis* falls prey to a giant squid. A pearl forms within another Mollusk class, the clam. Echinoderm starfish appear. Trilobites *Ampyx priscus* watch the conflict.

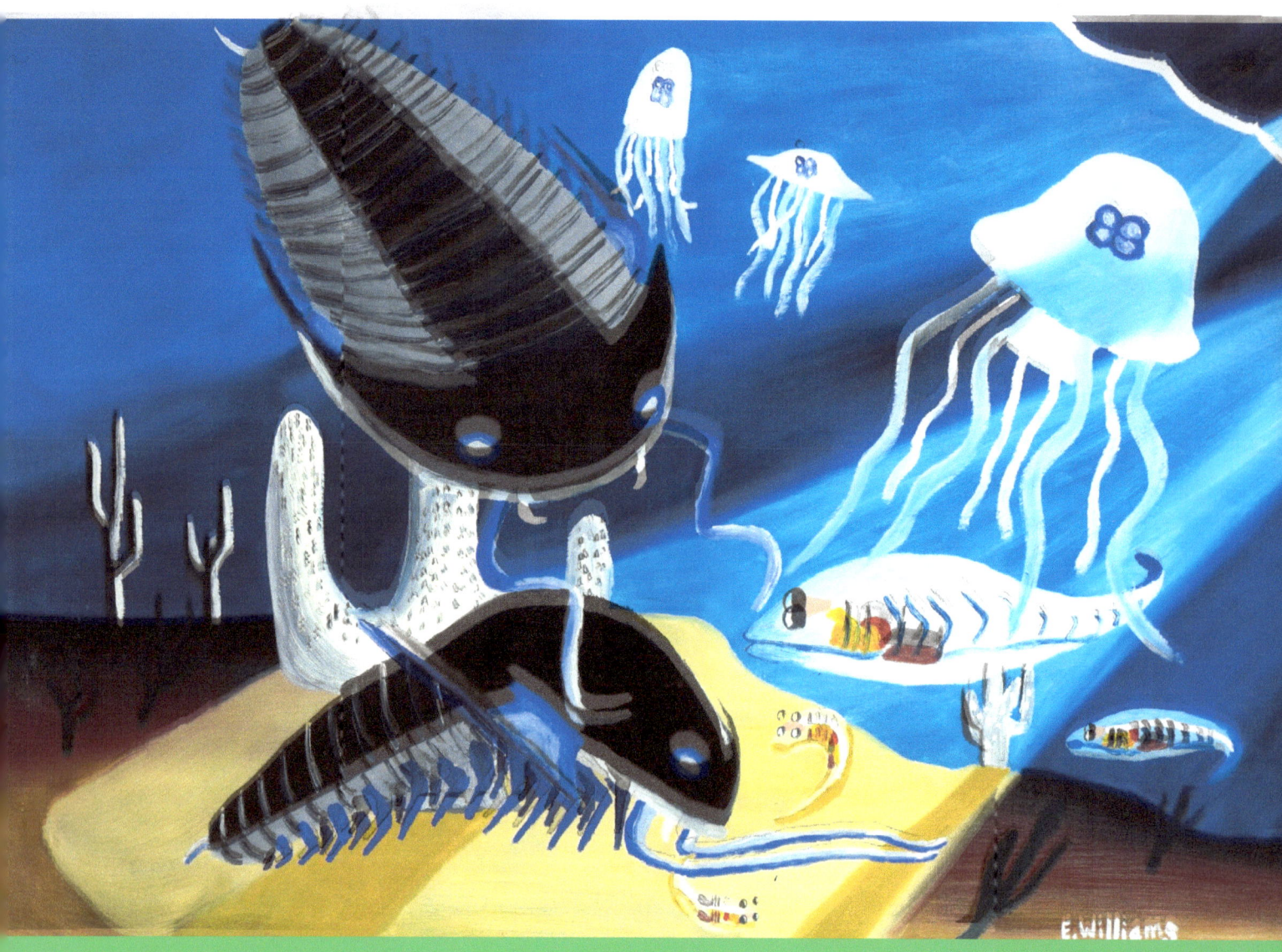

CAMBRIAN PERIOD

500 M.Y.A.
PHANEROZOIC EON
PALEOZOIC ERA

"Paradox"

True Vertebrates in the form of fish evolve from the Chordates. The giant Trilobite *Paradoxides paradoxissimus* preys upon one of the first primitive fish *Haikouichthys ercaicunensis*. Moonlight illuminates jellyfish and sponges.

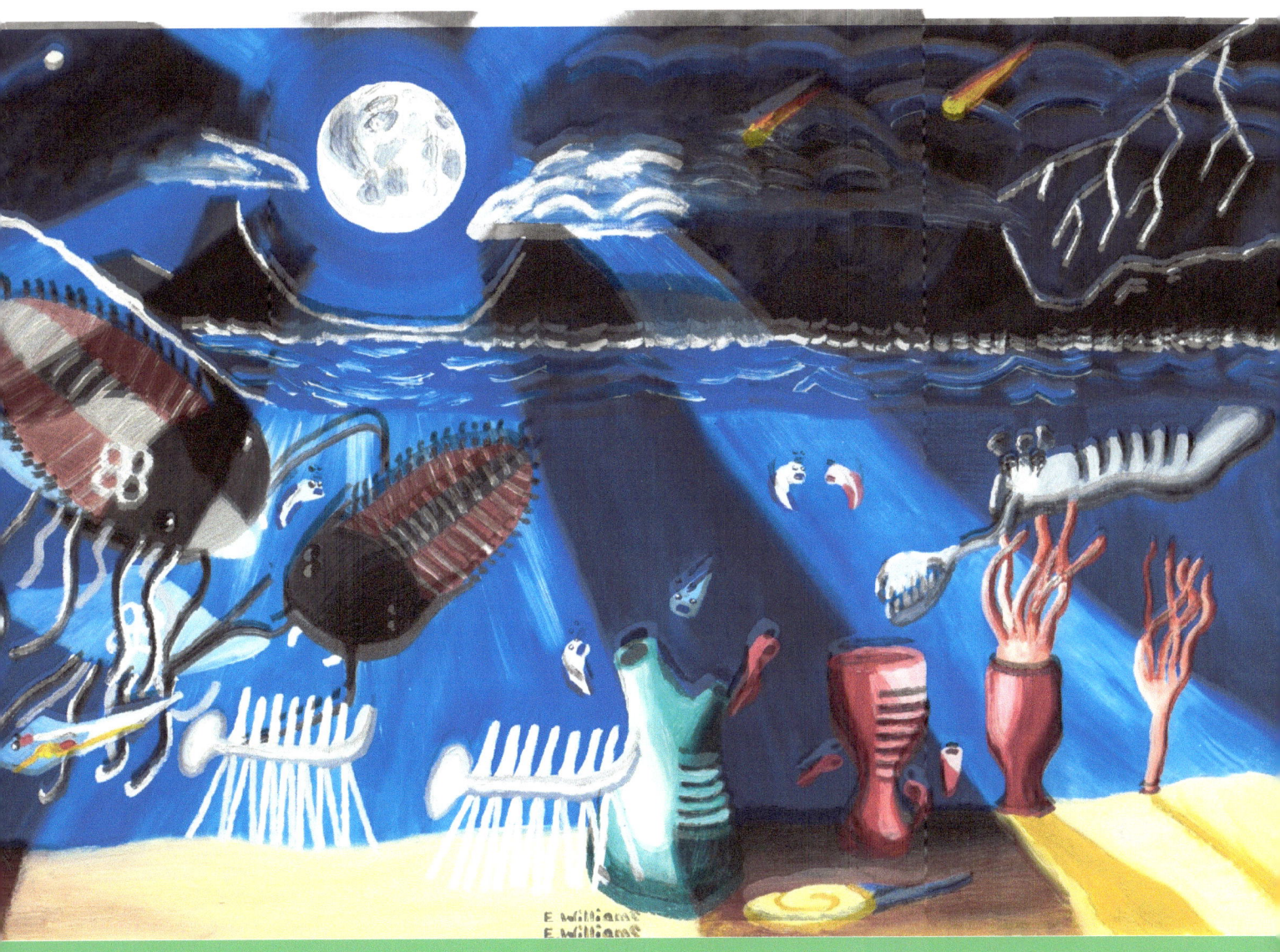

CAMBRIAN PERIOD

PALEOZOIC ERA

542 M.Y.A.

"Iapetus Ocean"

The Echinoderm sea lily *Echmatocrinus brachatus* and the Chordate sea squirt (Tunicate) *Shankouclava shankouense* evolve. Both their larval forms are free-swimming and resemble one another. These larvae bid farewell to each other as the Superphylum Deuterostome splits into the Echinoderm and Chordate phyla. Arthropod Trilobites dominate the sea for the first time, menacing the newly evolved free-swimming chordate *Pikaia gracilens*. Bizarre animals of unknown phyla or kingdoms dwell in the sea, including the spiny *Hallucigenia sparsa* and the swimming *Opabinia regalis*. The Moon appears larger in the sky due to its proximity.

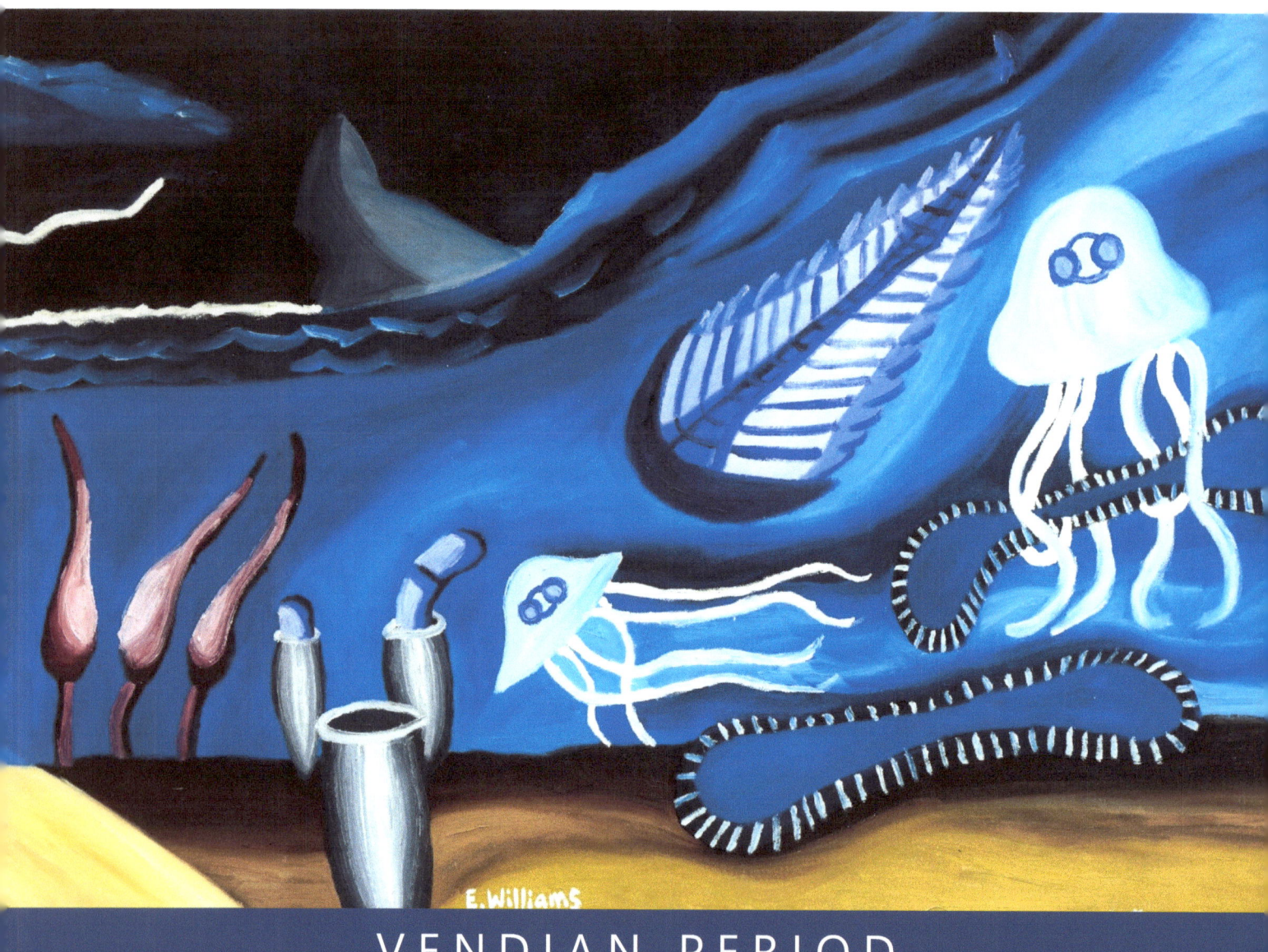

VENDIAN PERIOD

542 M.Y.A.
Proterozoic Eon

NEOPROTEROZOIC ERA

"Rise of Cnidaria"

The Cnidarian jellyfish evolve and prey upon *Kimberella quadrata*, frightening tube-worms back into their tubes. A *Spriggina floundersi* resembling an elongated Trilobite swims by. A possible ancestor to the sea pens *Charnia masoni* drifts in the currents.

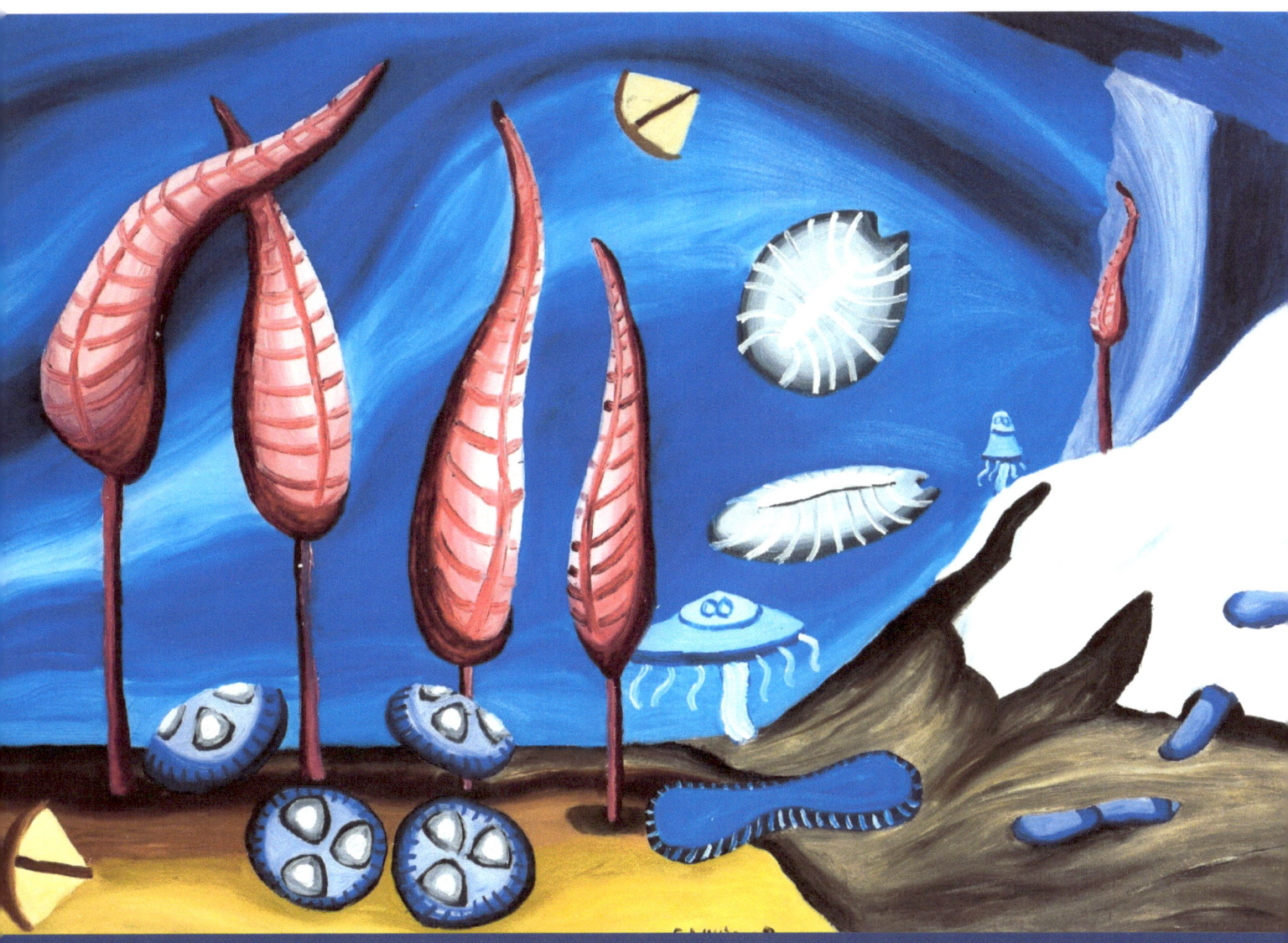

"Mystery Phyla"

Mysterious animal phyla (or a long extinct separate Kingdom of life) appear. Ribbed *Dickinsonia costata* swim above ancestors to Cnidarian jellyfish anchored to the sea bottom, while *Kimberella quadrata* swims below them. The three-lobed *Tribrachidium heraldicum* feed under *Charnia masoni*. Wedge-shaped *Parvancorina minchami* drift by.

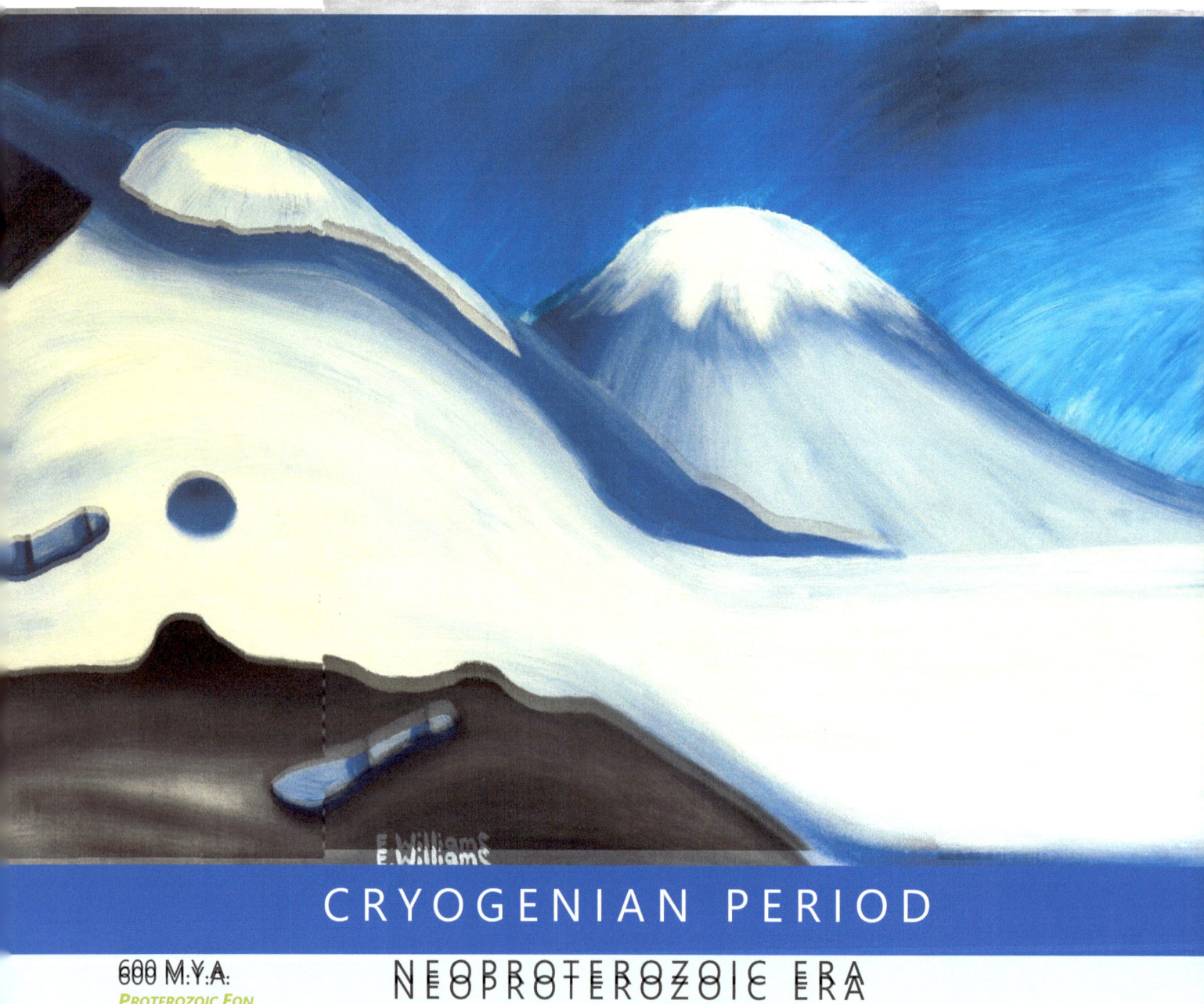

CRYOGENIAN PERIOD

600 M.Y.A.:
PROTEROZOIC EON

NEOPROTEROZOIC ERA

"Kingdom of Animalia"

Animal life, multicellular heterotrophs relying on digestion for energy, appear in the form of simple worm-like creatures. These proto-worms are the ancestors of the bilaterally symmetrical superphyla Protostomes (including the arthropod and mollusk phyla, whose first embryonic opening becomes the mouth) and Deuterostomes (including the Echinoderm and Chordate/Vertebrate phyla, whose first embryonic opening becomes the anus); and possibly the radially symmetrical Cnidaria. These creatures emerge from the frozen waste of the Cryogenian, the beginning of their kingdom on Earth.

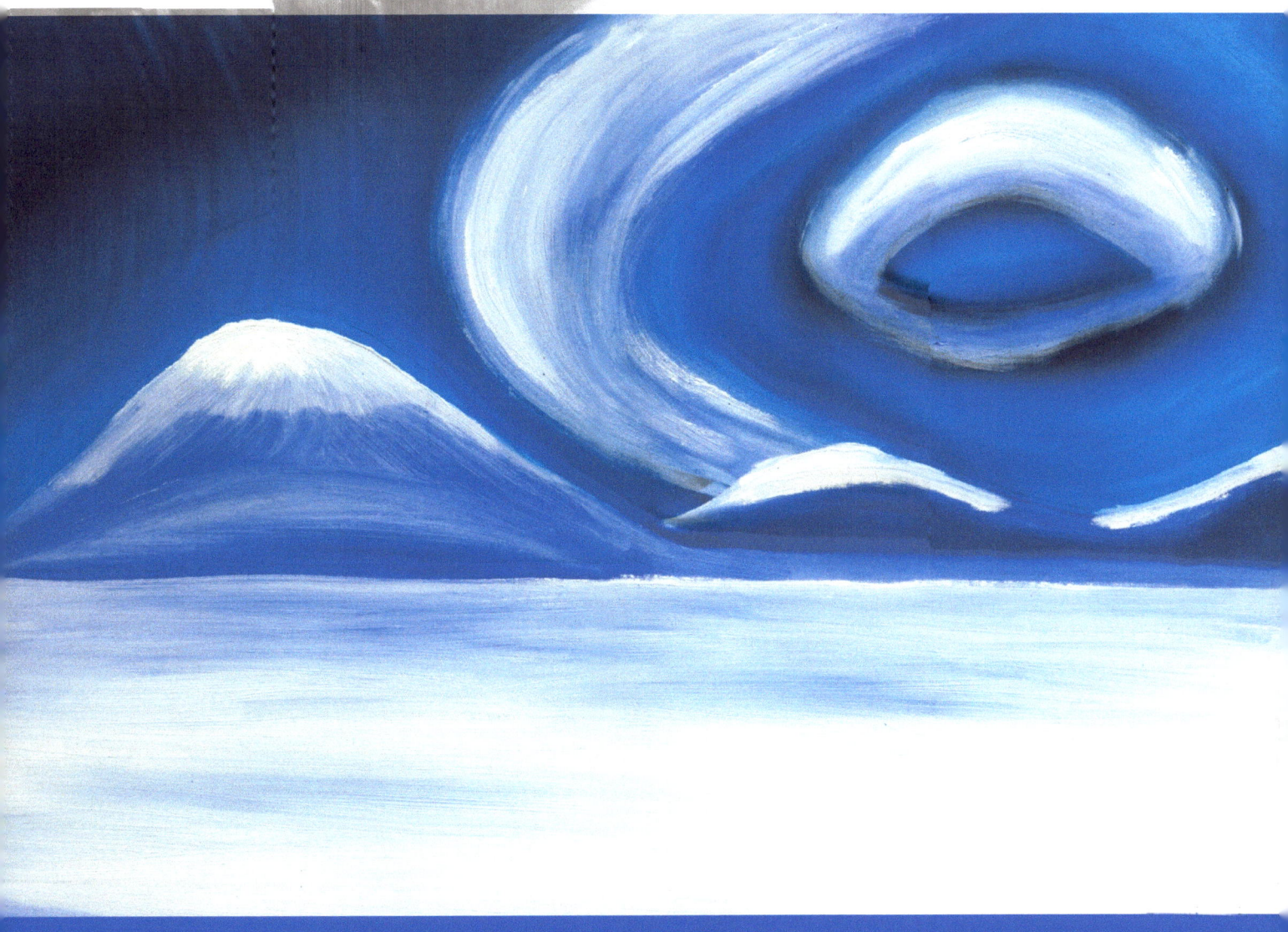

CRYOGENIAN PERIOD

NEOPROTEROZOIC ERA

850 M.Y.A.

"Snowball Earth part II"

Earth is a frozen wasteland, possibly all across the globe, in this second Snowball Earth episode.

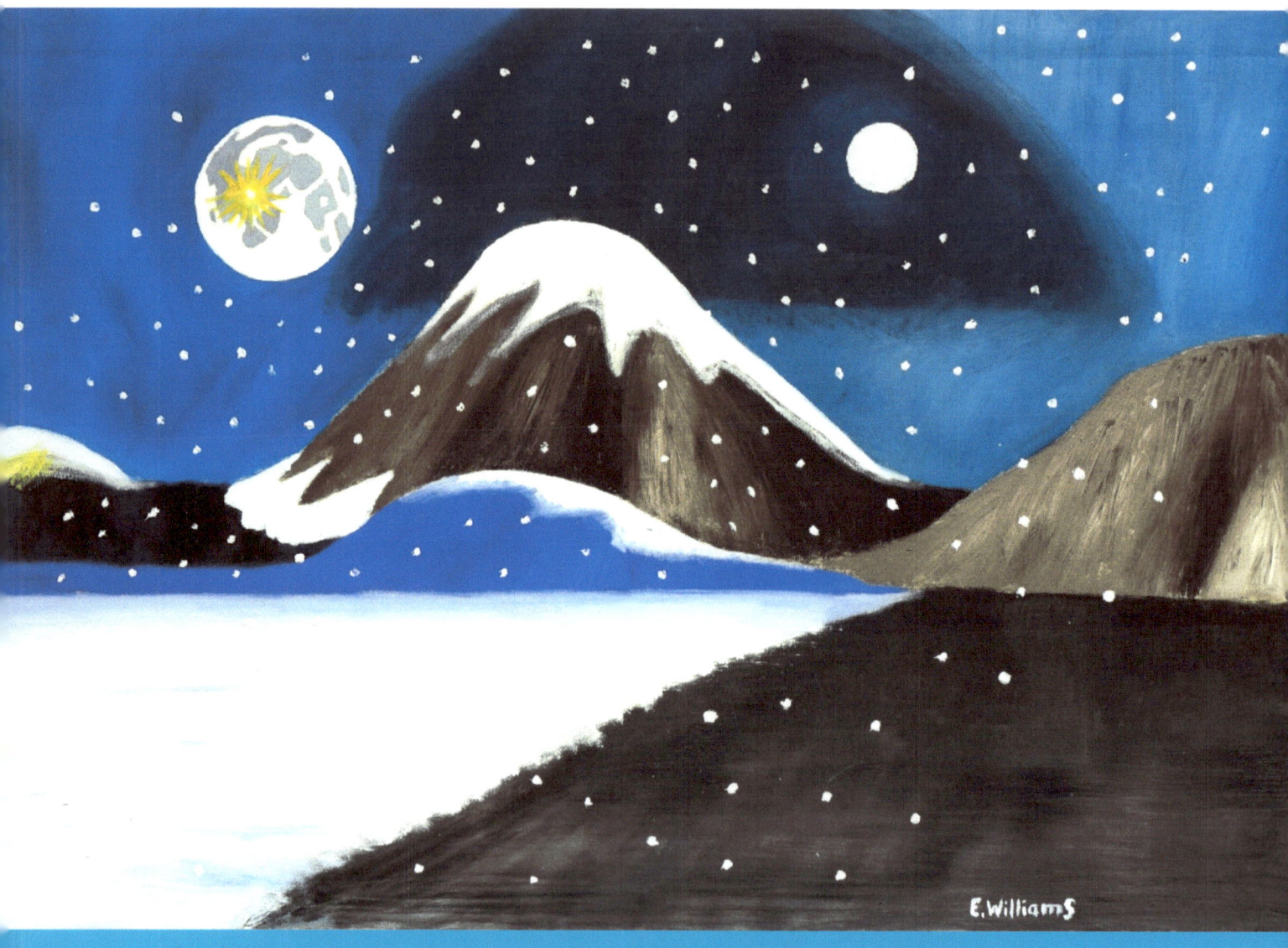

TONIAN PERIOD

850 M.Y.A.
PROTEROZOIC EON

NEOPROTEROZOIC ERA

"Copernicus"

The Copernicus impact on the Moon is visible in the daylight sky. The dim Sun can be seen behind a cloud, as Earth falls into one of its largest Ice Ages. The supercontinent Rodinia begins to break apart.

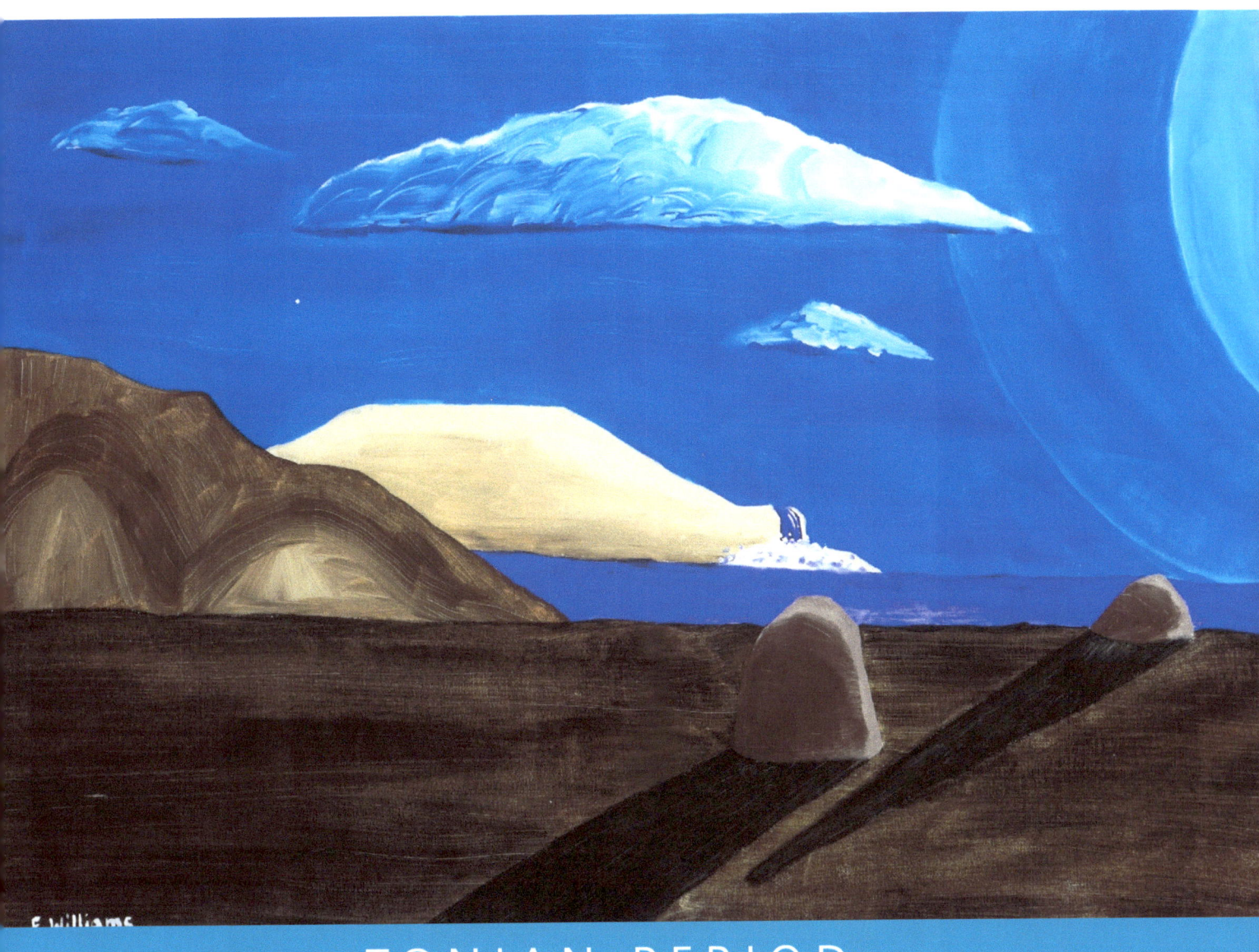

"Midnight in Rodinia part II"

A distant waterfall breaks up the desolation in this scene of Rodinia.

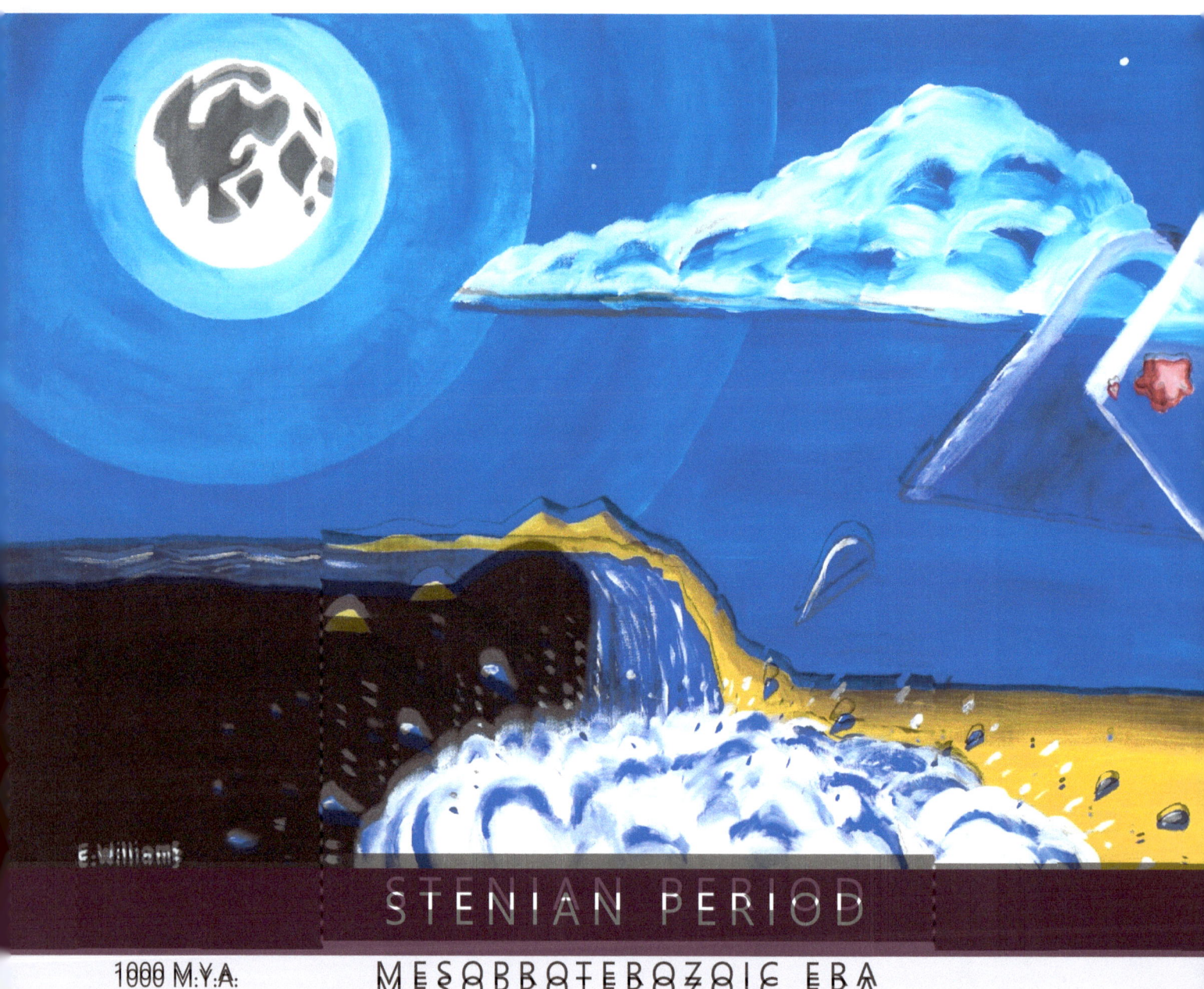

STENIAN PERIOD

1000 M.Y.A. MESOPROTEROZOIC ERA
PROTEROZOIC EON

"Midnight in Rodinia part I"

A closer waterfall is illuminated by a large full Moon in the supercontinent Rodinia. There is still no life on land. Our scene becomes magnified in a droplet of this waterfall, revealing microscopic life teeming in the Stenian seas...

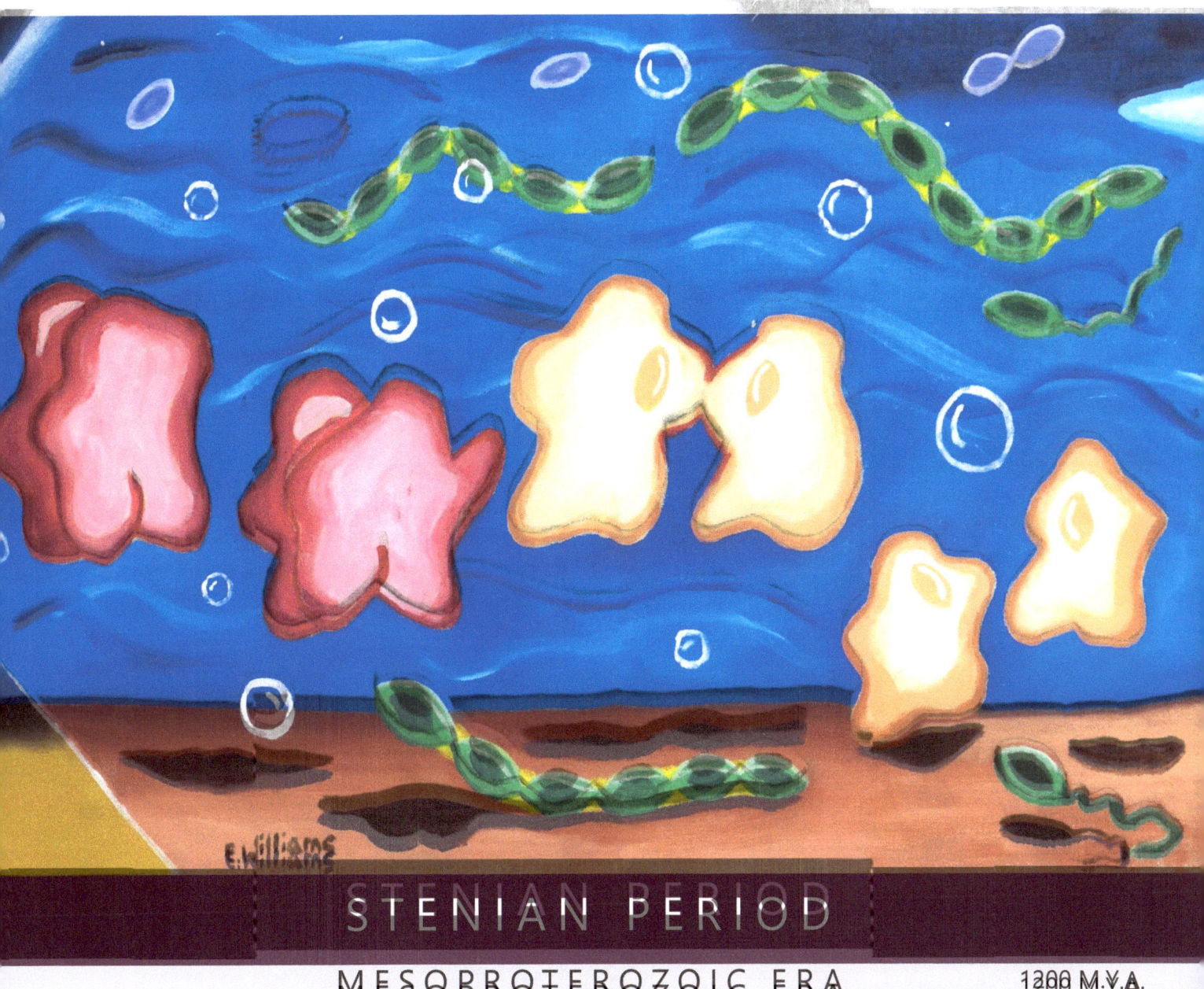

STENIAN PERIOD

MESOPROTEROZOIC ERA — 1200 M.Y.A.

"Love Dance"

Sexual reproduction develops in the Eukaryotes, allowing a greater degree of genetic diversification. Asexual Prokaryotes look on jealously as multicellular algae drift by.

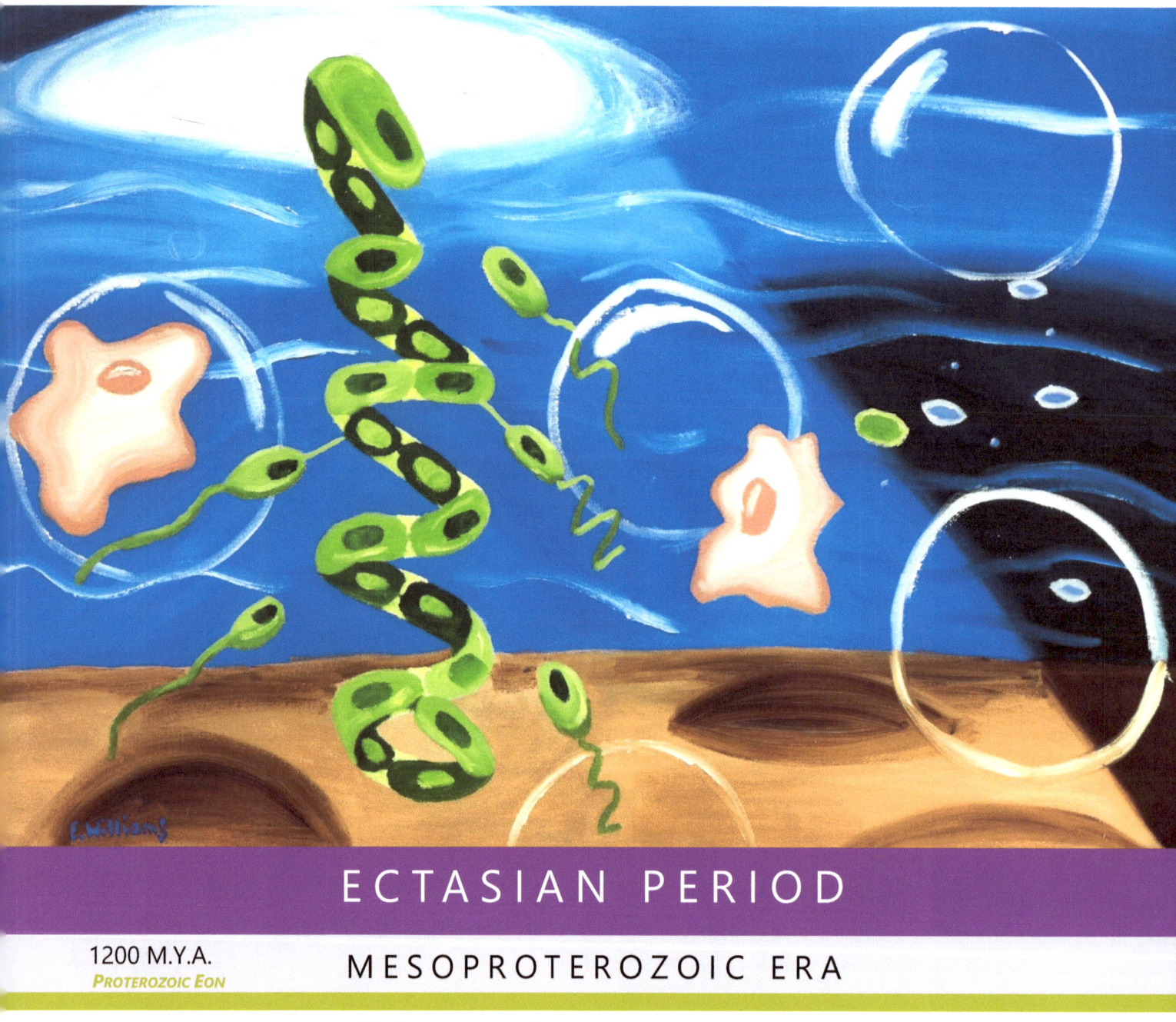

ECTASIAN PERIOD

1200 M.Y.A.
PROTEROZOIC EON

MESOPROTEROZOIC ERA

"Cellular Teamwork (Join Together in the Band)"

Photosynthetic eukaryotes band together to form the first multicellular organism, the algae *Grypania spiralis*. Some Eukaryotes and the Prokaryotes opt out, preferring their unicellular independence. The supercontinent Nuna begins to break apart.

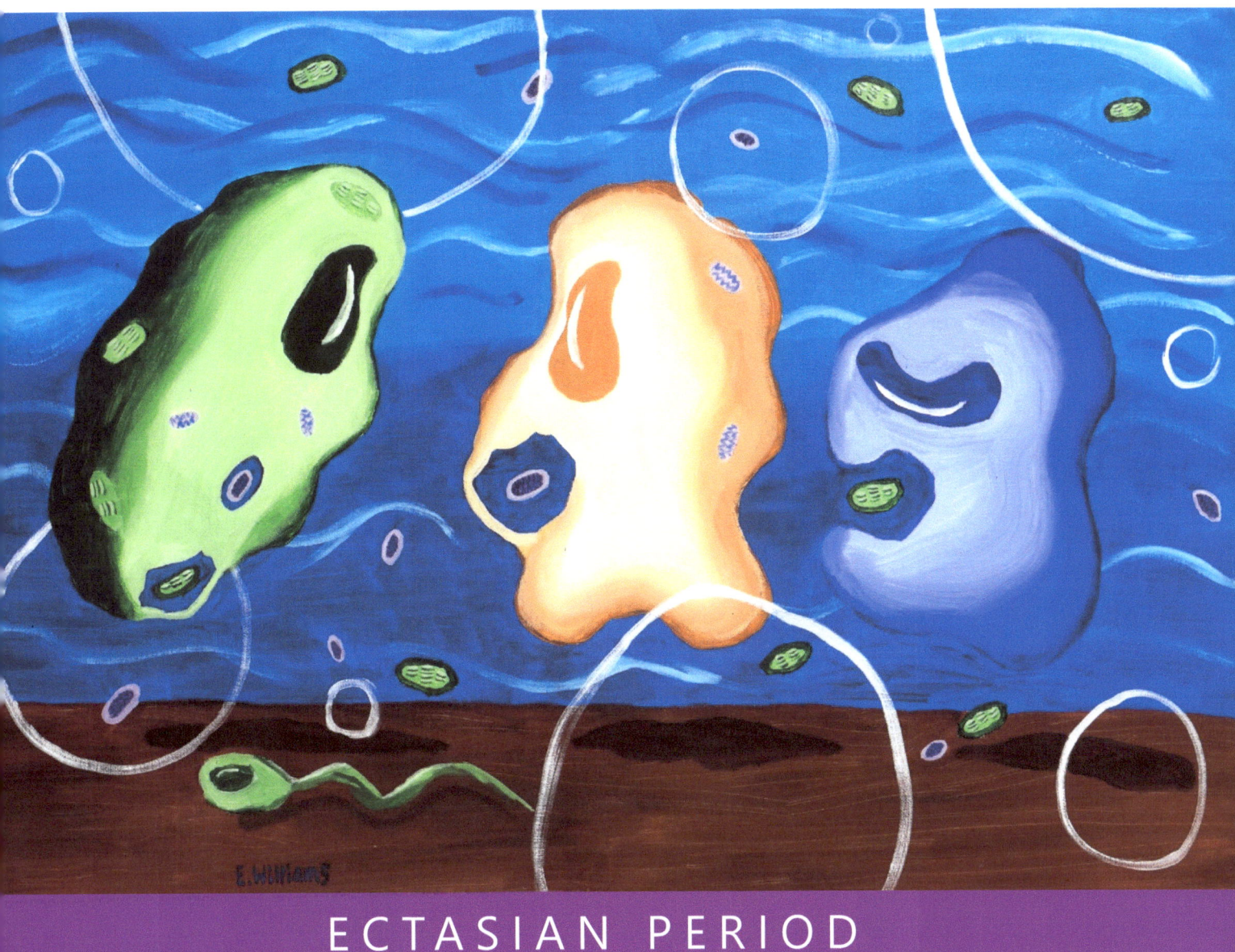

ECTASIAN PERIOD

MESOPROTEROZOIC ERA

1400 M.Y.A.

"Symbiosis Event"

Eukaryotic cells envelop purple nonsulfur bacteria, which become organelles called mitochondria. The first ancestral plant cell absorbs both this purple nonsulfur bacteria and a cyanobacteria, which becomes a chloroplast. Both these organelles retain genetic material, and pass this on through the ages. Mitochondria enable cells to oxidize sugars to carbon dioxide, releasing more energy than through anaerobic fermentation. Chloroplasts enable the eukaryotes that carry them to become autotrophic, capable of making sugars from carbon dioxide using sunlight.

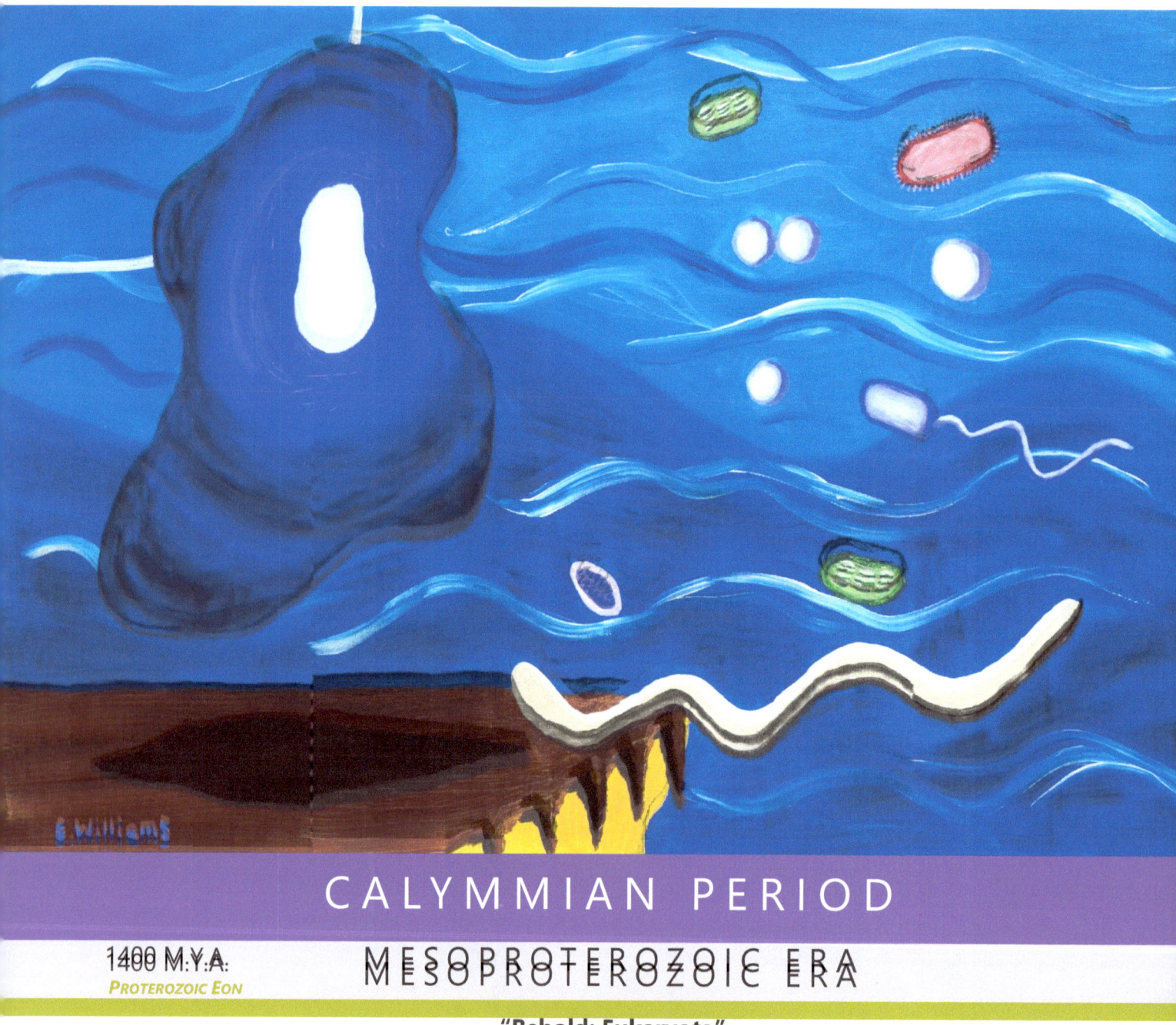

CALYMMIAN PERIOD

1400 M.Y.A.
PROTEROZOIC EON

MESOPROTEROZOIC ERA

"Behold: Eukaryota"

The first Eukaryote cell that compartmentalizes its genetic material into a nucleus develops, with a variety of Prokaryotic bacteria bearing witness.

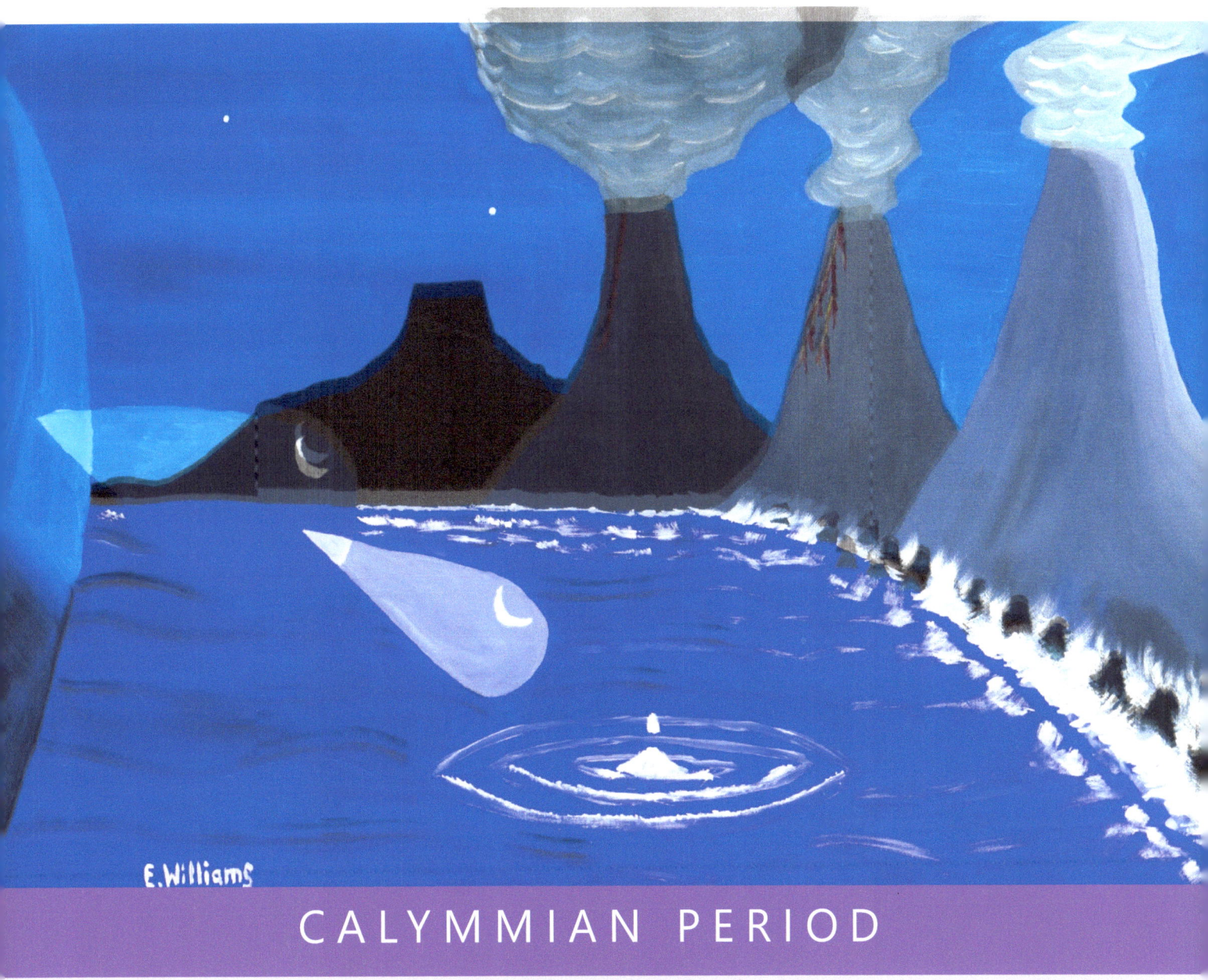

CALYMMIAN PERIOD

MESOPROTEROZOIC ERA   1600 M.Y.A.

"Continent Building"

Geologic platform covers, relatively flat areas of plates, expand and are created in this volcanically active scene from the Calymmian. Stromatolites are visible on the shoreline.

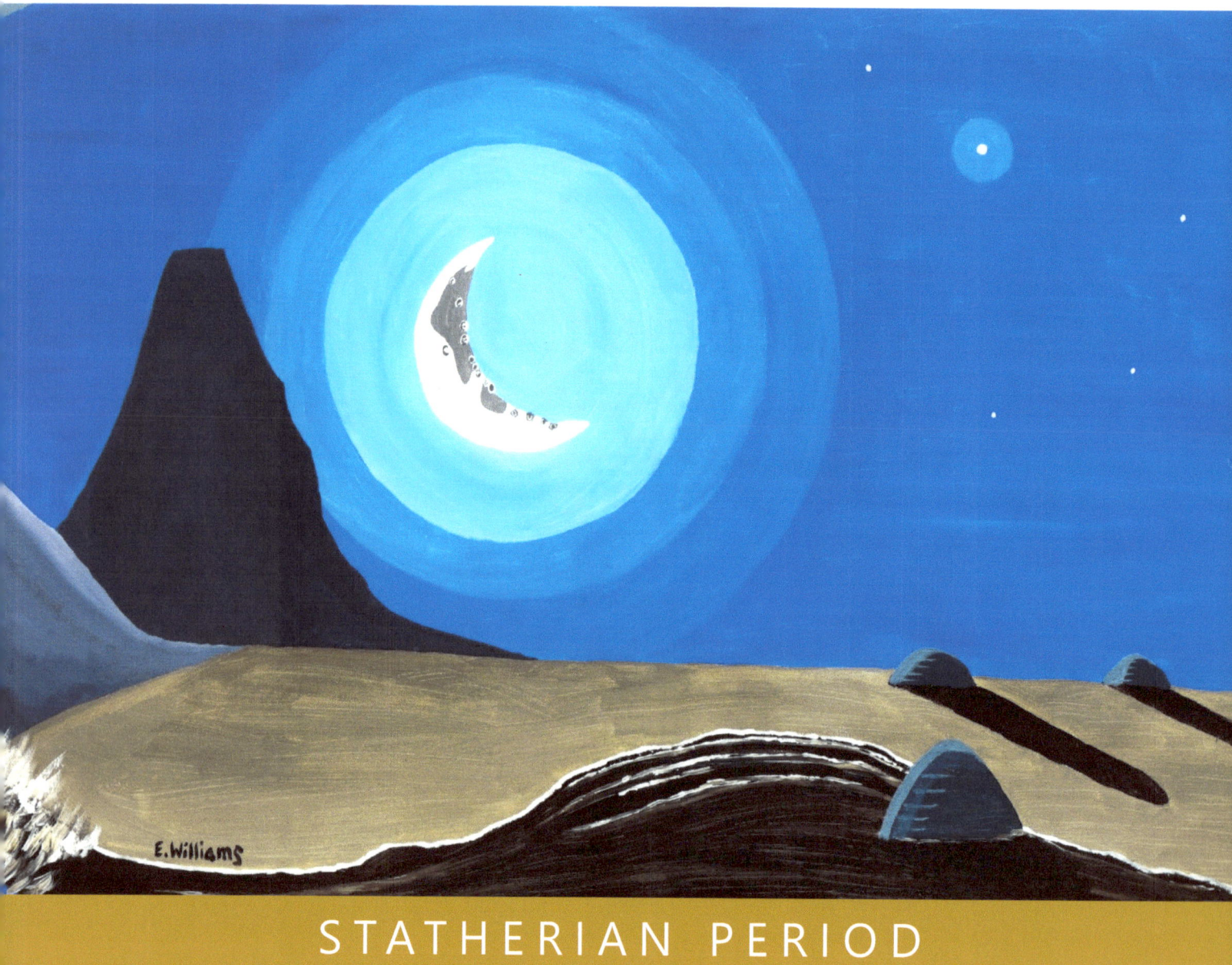

STATHERIAN PERIOD

1600 M.Y.A.
Proterozoic Eon

PALEOPROTEROZOIC ERA

"Midnight in Nuna part II"

The crescent Moon appears large in the Statherian sky over Nuna due to its close proximity. No one witnesses the long shadows cast on the Statherian wastelands.

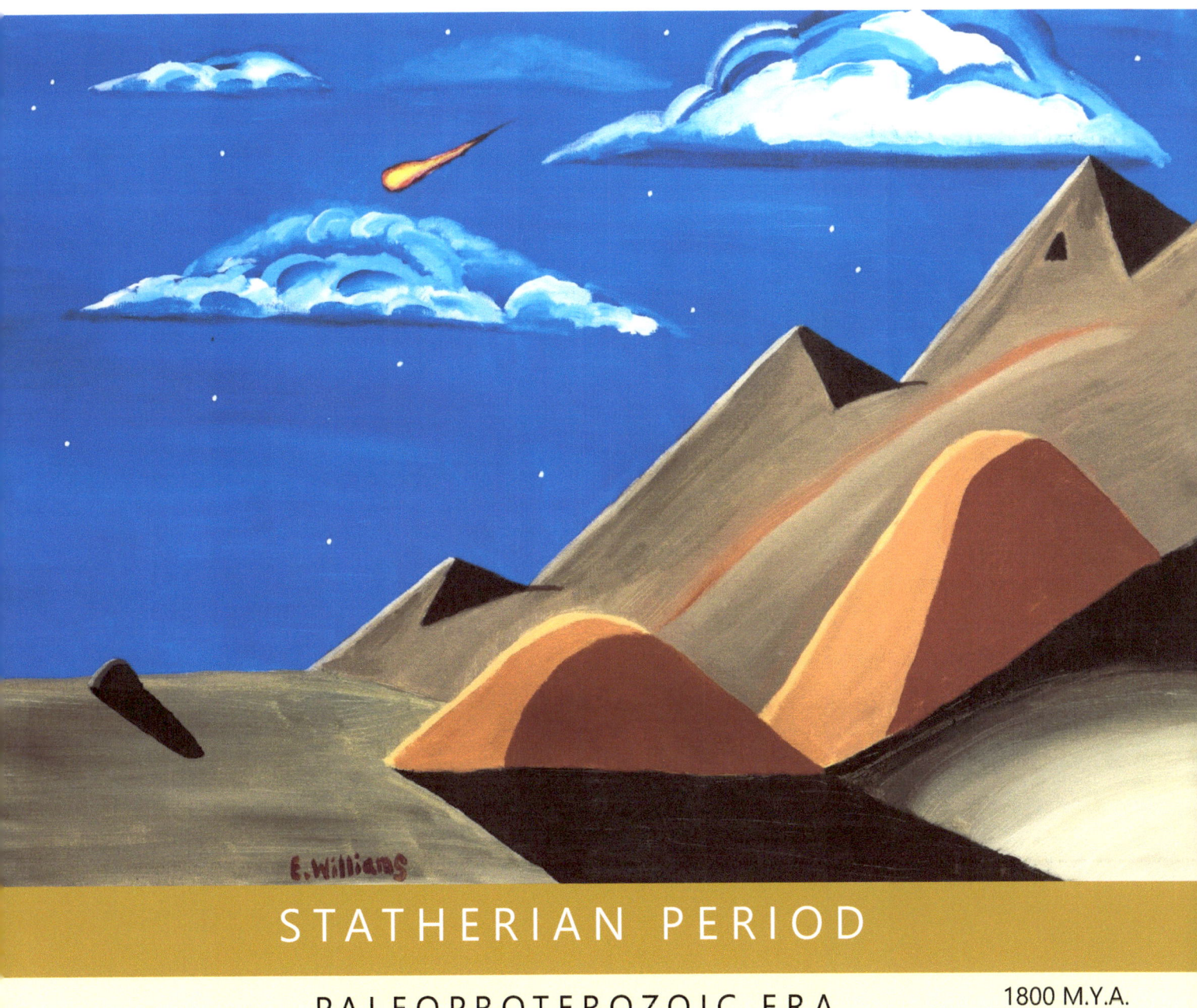

STATHERIAN PERIOD

PALEOPROTEROZOIC ERA   1800 M.Y.A.

"Midnight in Nuna part I"

The supercontinent Nuna forms in this midnight scene of desolation. A comet appears in the Statherian sky.

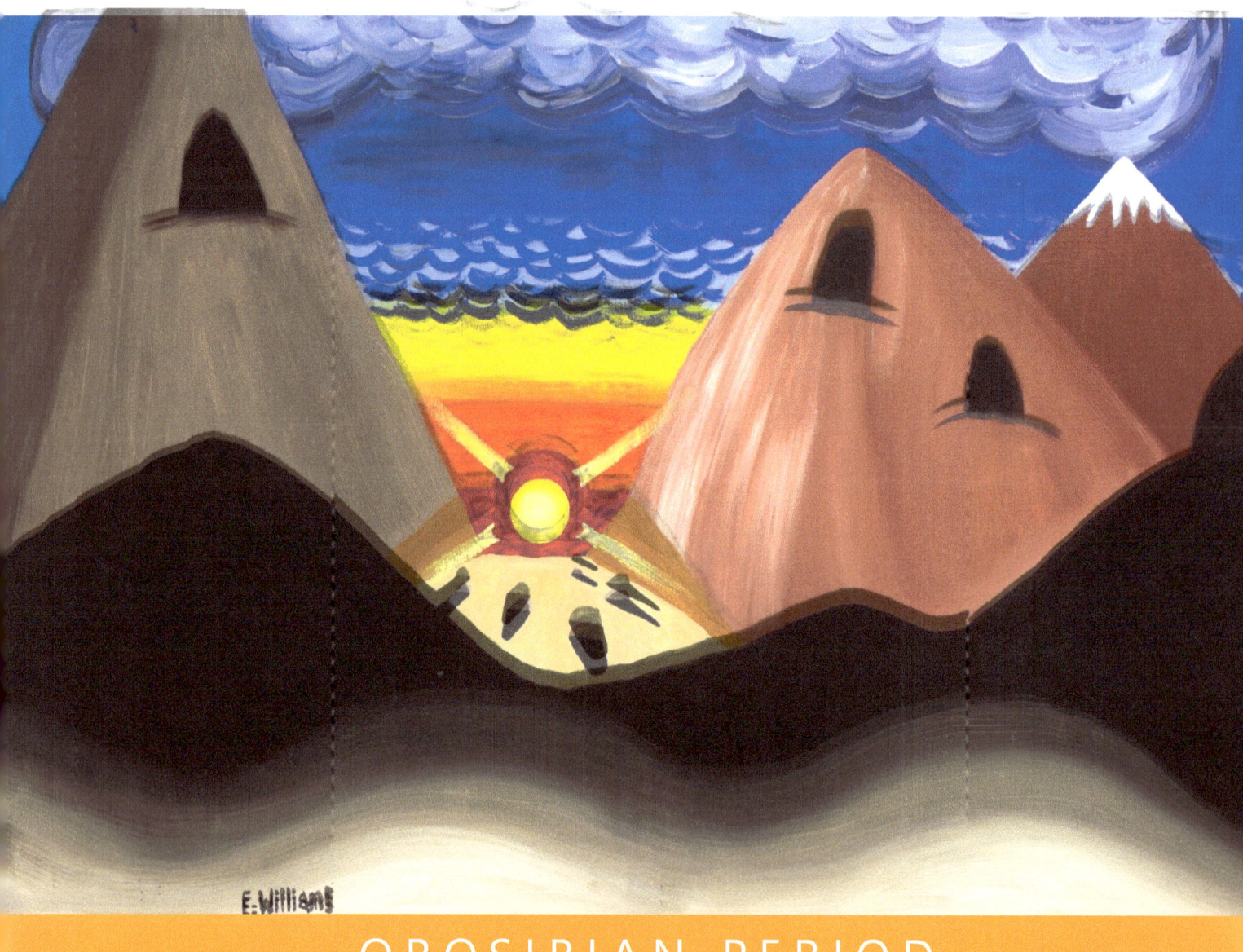

OROSIRIAN PERIOD

1800 M.Y.A.
Proterozoic Eon

PALEOPROTEROZOIC ERA

"Mountain Building"

Tectonic plates push against one another, creating vast mountain ranges on the Earth.

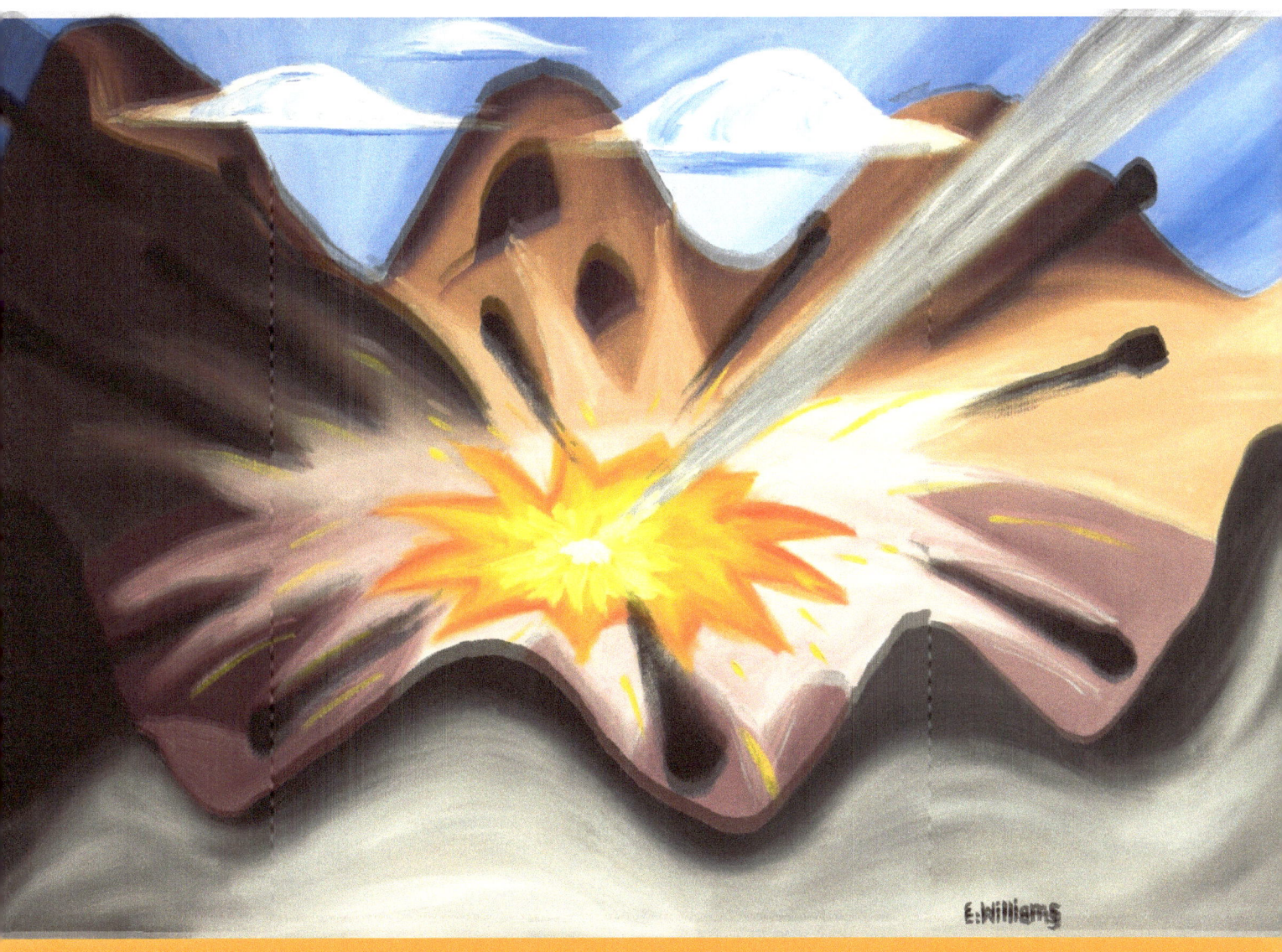

OROSIRIAN PERIOD

PALEOPROTEROZOIC ERA — 2050 M.Y.A.

"Vredefort Impact"

A nine-mile-wide asteroid strikes the Earth. This Vredefort impact, the largest verified in history, occurs without witnesses in the barren Orosirian landscape.

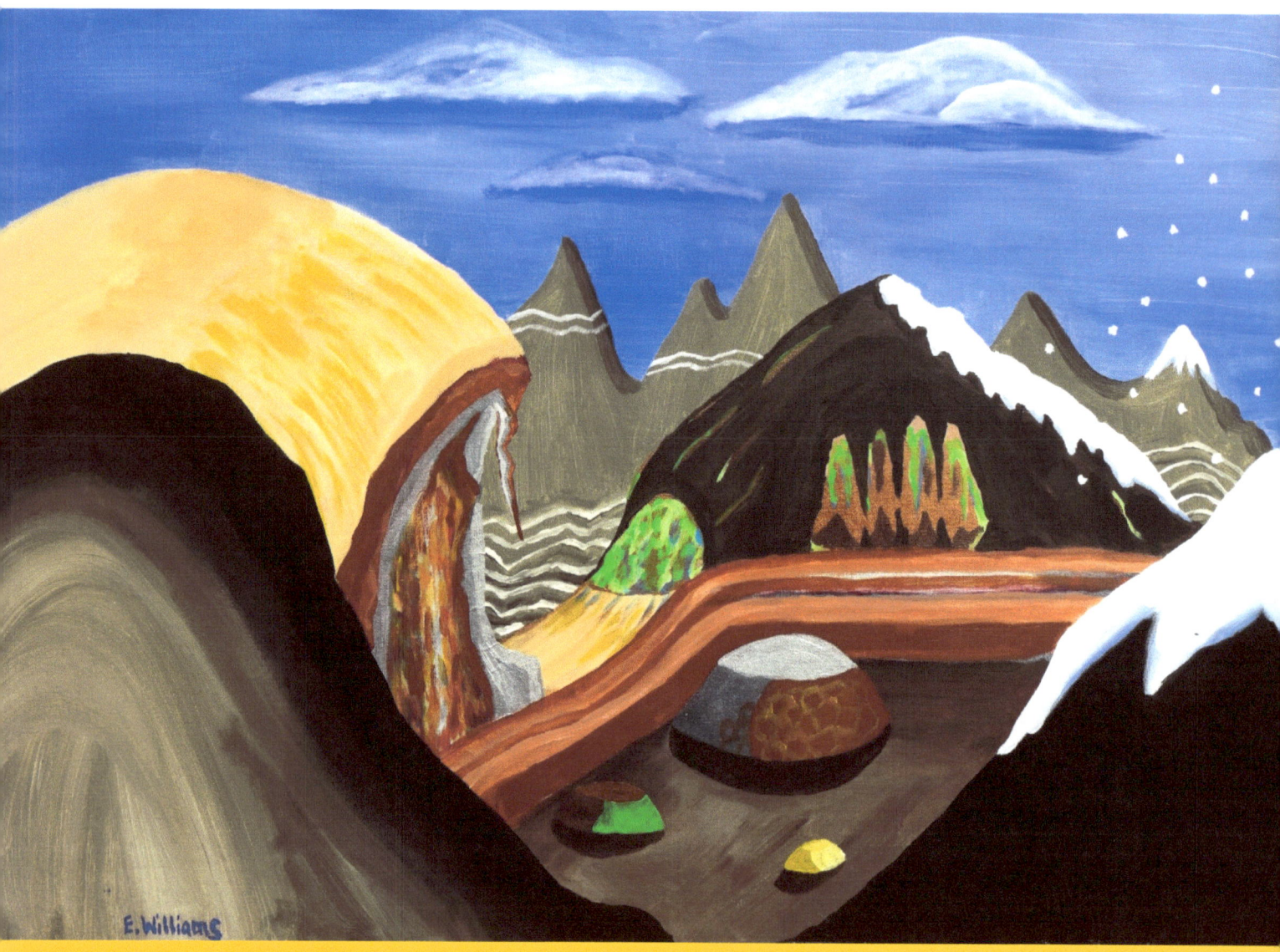

RHYACIAN PERIOD

2050 M.Y.A.
Proterozoic Eon

PALEOPROTEROZOIC ERA

"Rust"

Cyanobacteria have produced sufficient oxygen for iron to rust, visible as geological "red beds." Copper and aluminum deposits also oxidize in this newly reactive atmosphere.

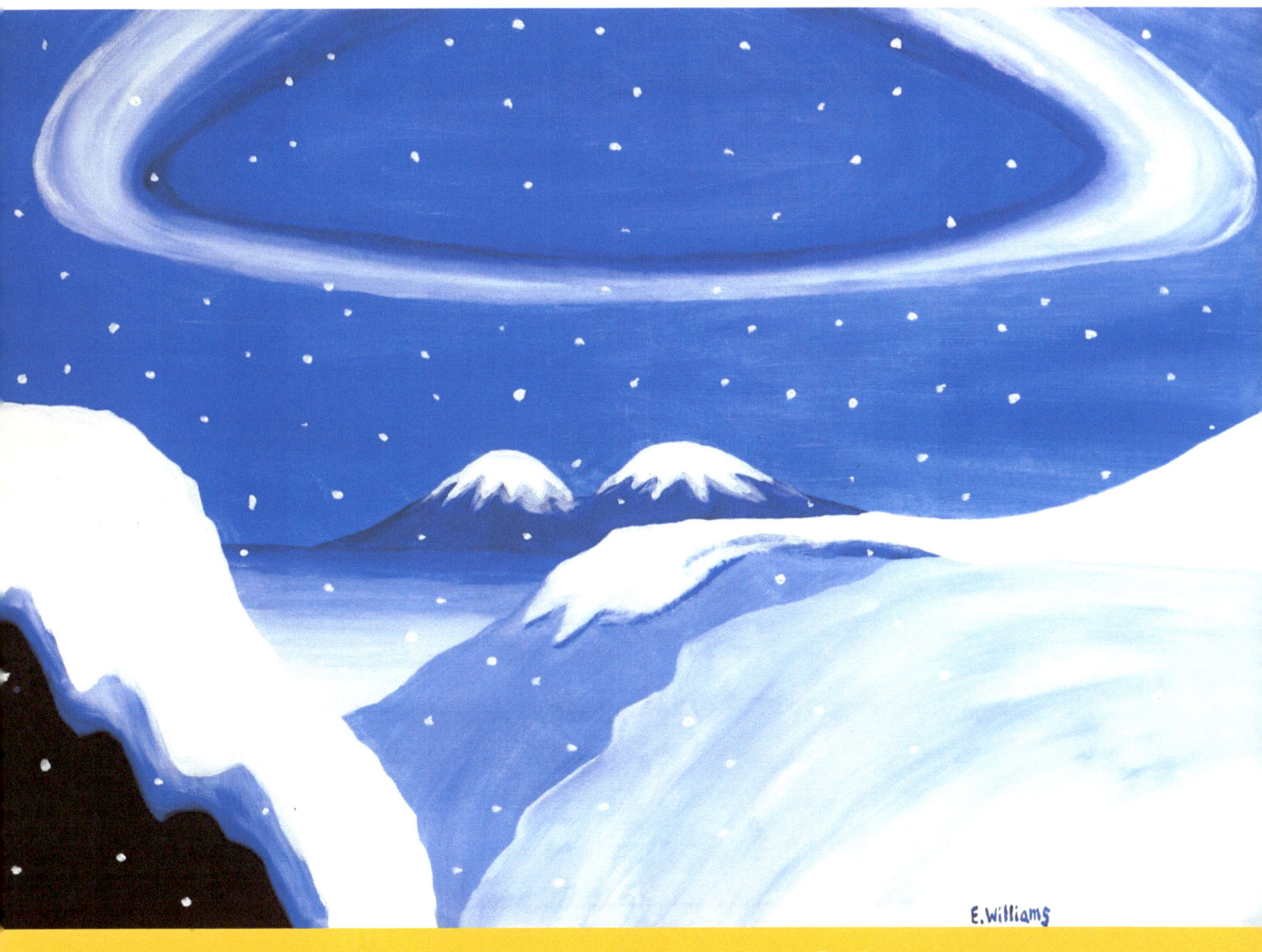

RHYACIAN PERIOD

PALEOPROTEROZOIC ERA — 2300 M.Y.A.

"Snowball Earth part I"

Earth is a frozen wasteland in this Rhyacian scene.

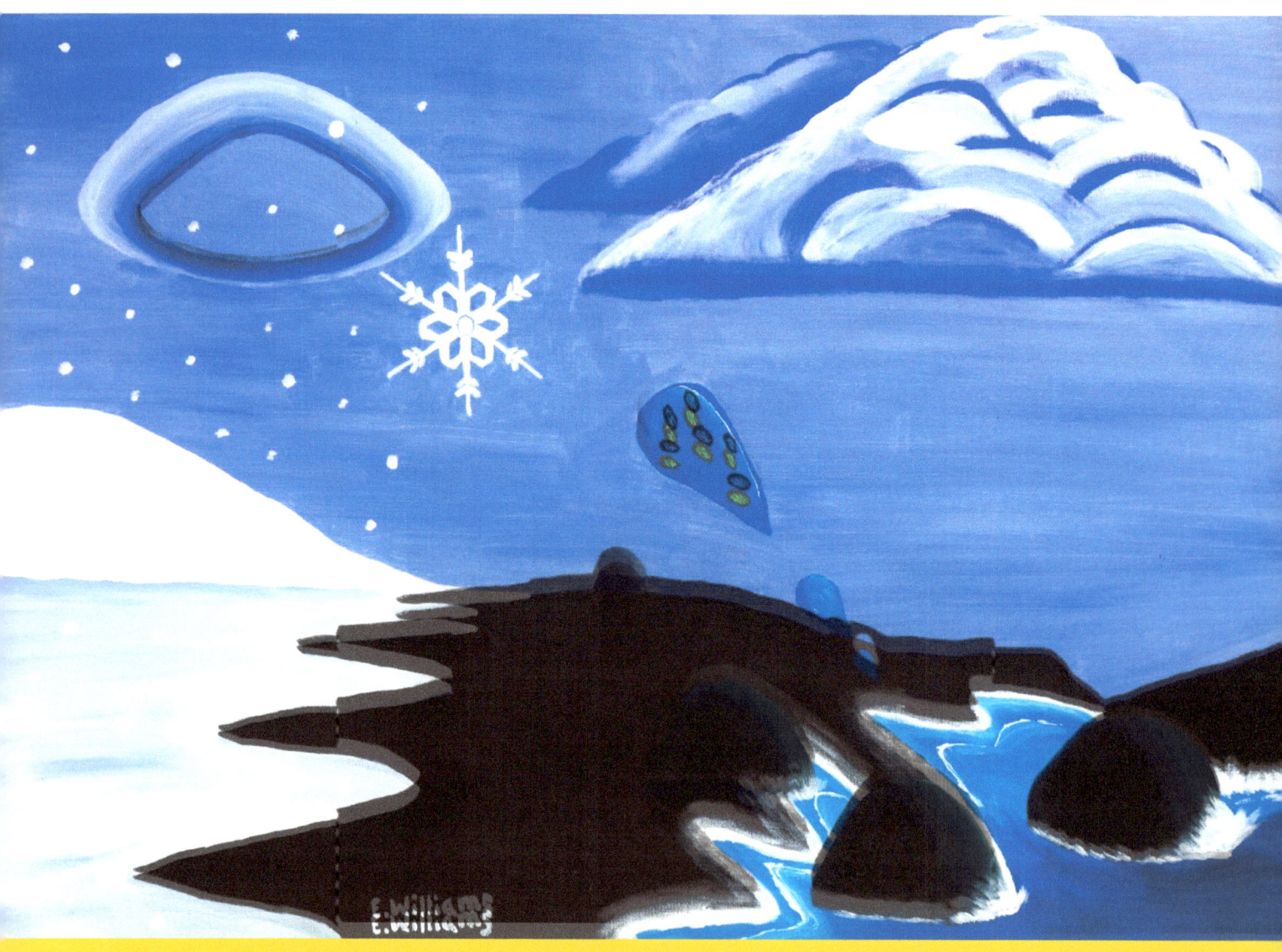

SIDERIAN PERIOD

2300 M.Y.A: PALEOPROTEROZOIC ERA
Proterozoic Eon

"Oxygen Holocaust"

Cyanobacteria have produced a sufficient amount of oxygen to oxidize methane, generating the weaker greenhouse gas carbon dioxide. This initiates the longest Ice Age in Earth's history, and the first of two where possibly its entire surface is frozen. Mass extinctions of anaerobic bacteria occur from the climatic and atmospheric change caused by Cyanobacteria.

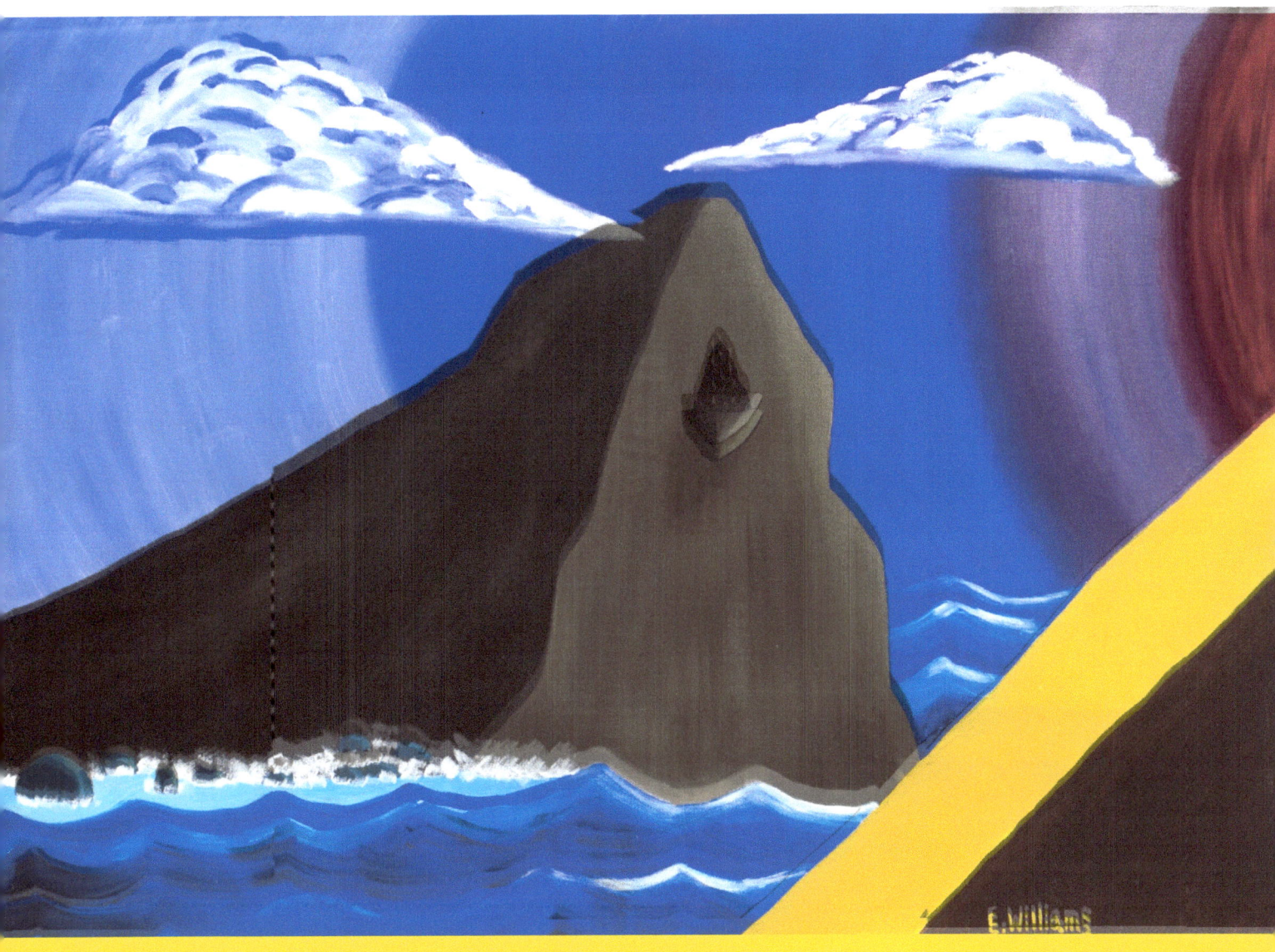

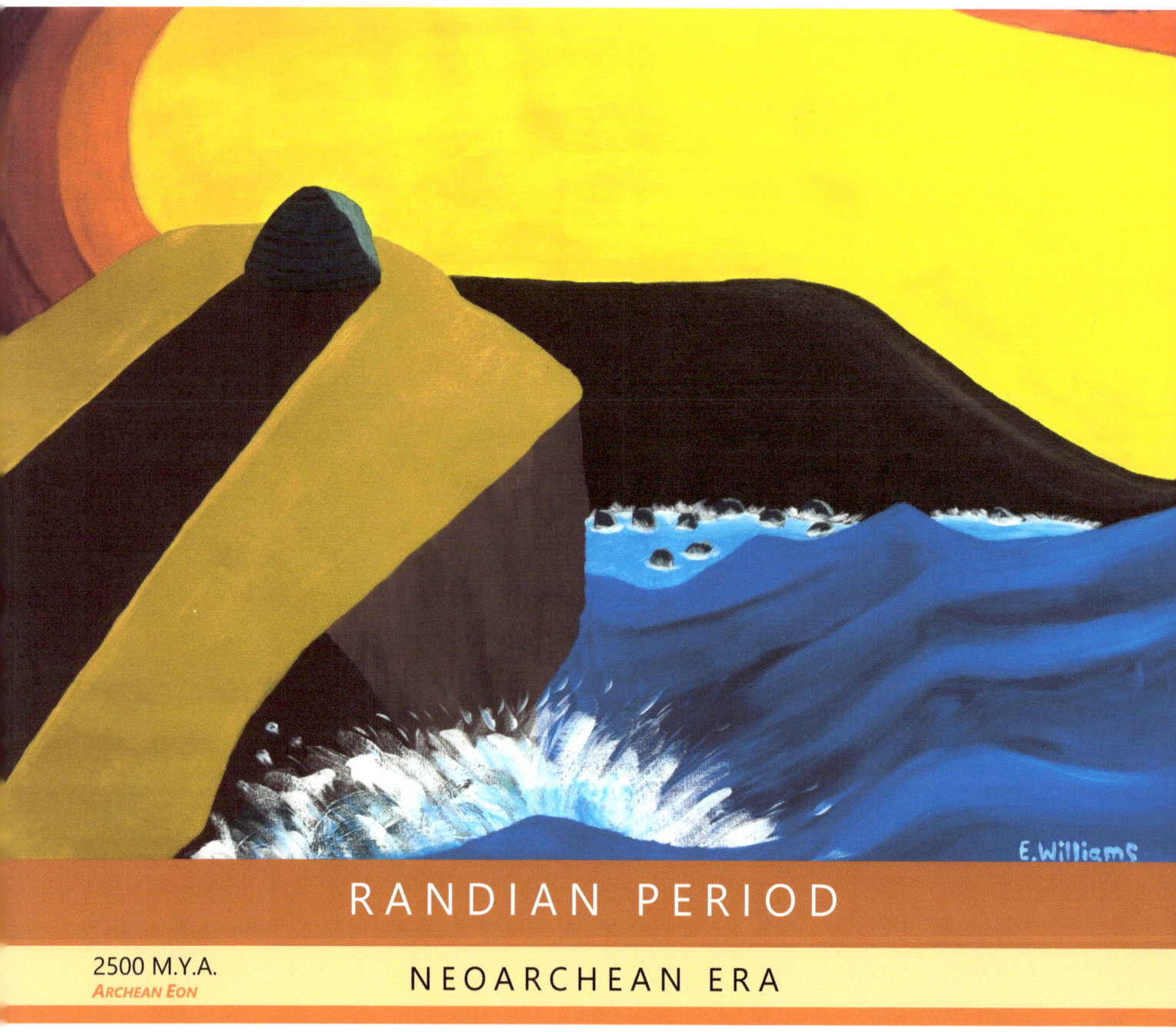

RANDIAN PERIOD

2500 M.Y.A.
ARCHEAN EON

NEOARCHEAN ERA

"Great Canyon (Plates) part I"

Continents form, as Ur begins to split apart through plate tectonics. Cyanobacteria thrive in shallow seas, banding together in mats with integrated minerals to form structures called stromatolites. A stromatolite observes the Sun over the canyon between newly formed land masses.

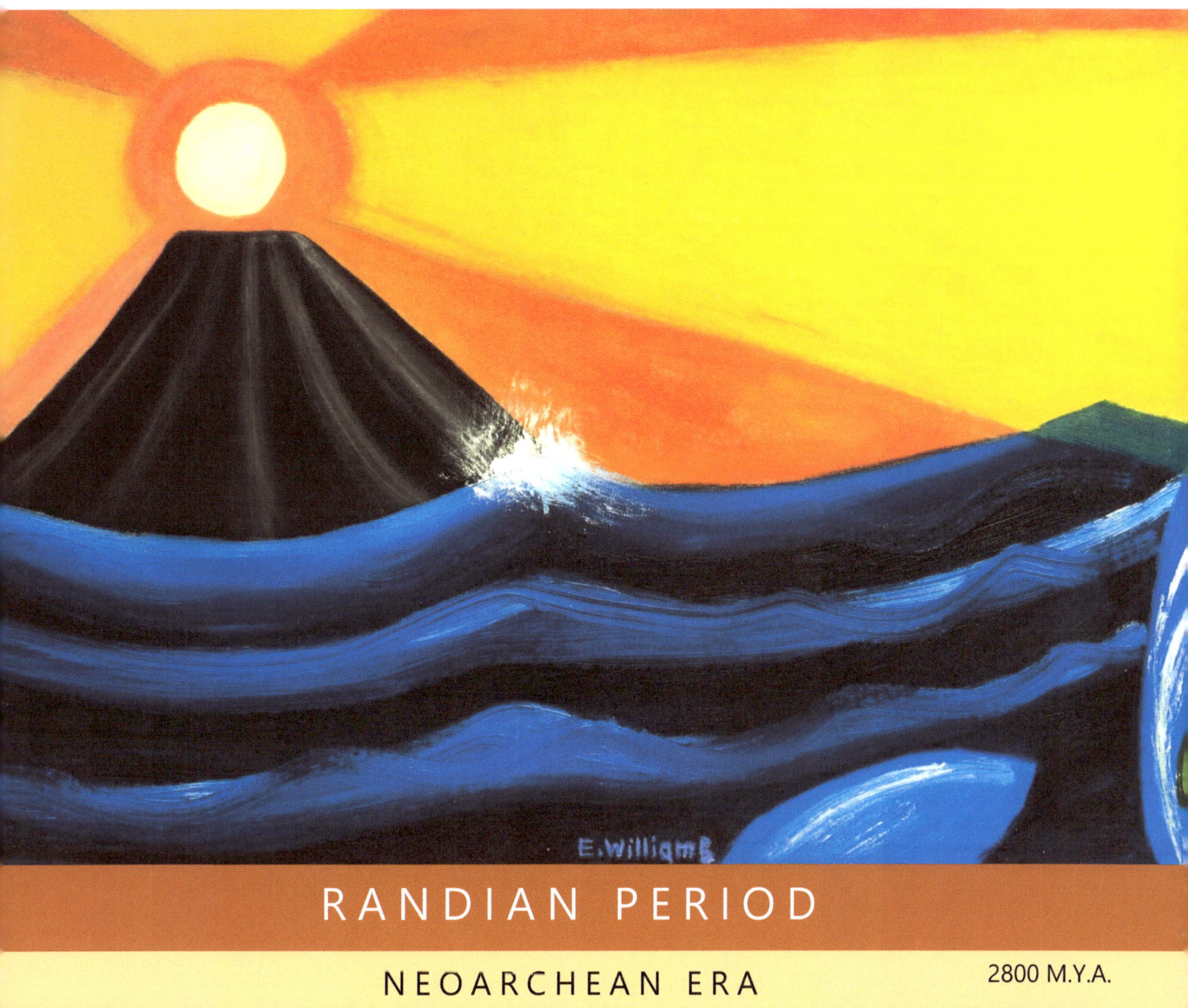

"Ur"

The first supercontinent Ur appears; it is the first and only land mass on Earth at this time. The Earth is no longer a Waterworld.

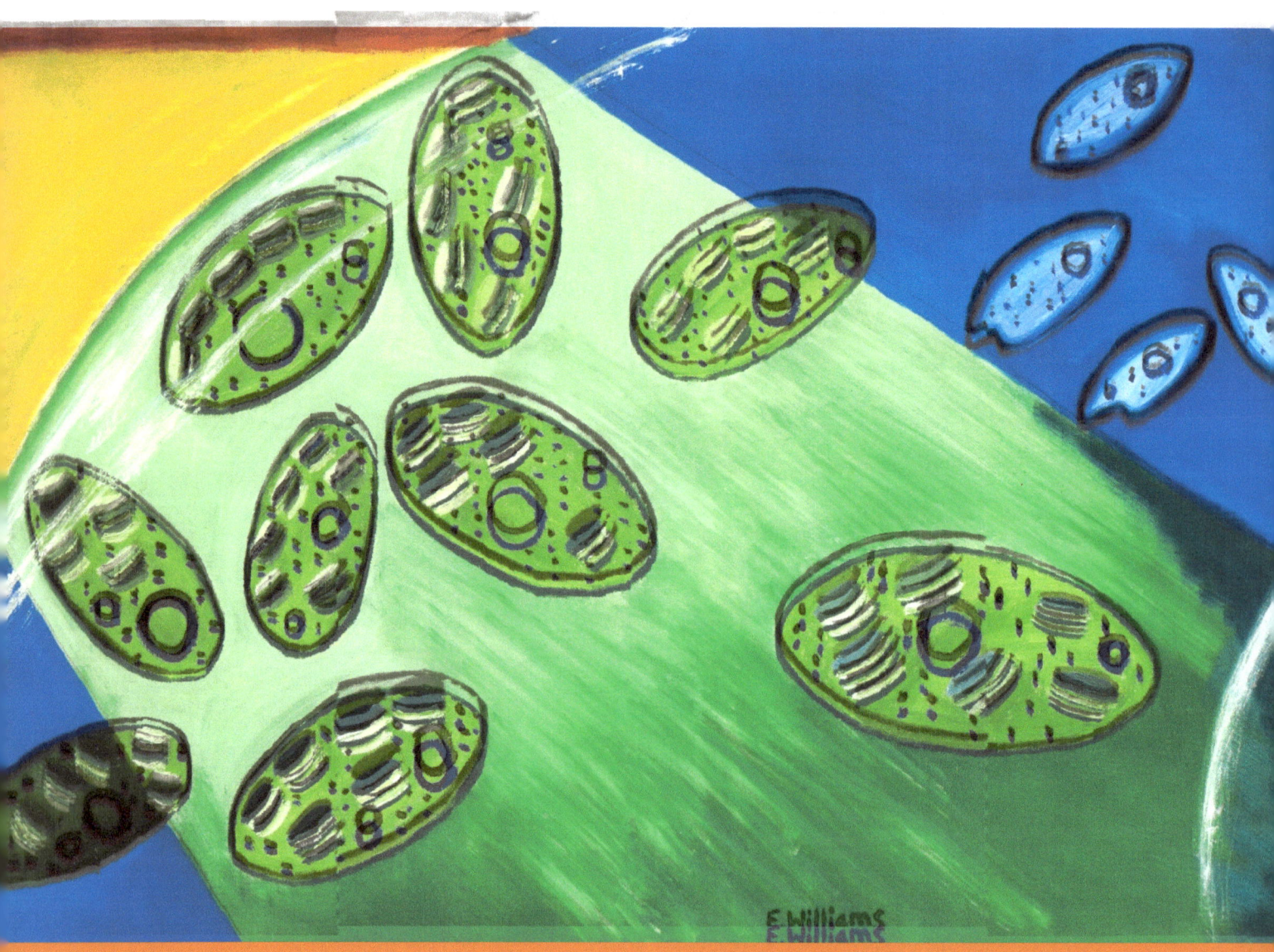

SWAZIAN PERIOD

2800 M.Y.A.
ARCHEAN EON

MESOARCHEAN ERA

"Autotroph"

Blue-green algae, which are actually photosynthetic bacteria called Cyanobacteria, evolve and become the first autotrophic organisms capable of making their own food. We can think of Cyanobacteria roughly as free-living chloroplasts. Their ability to fix carbon dioxide into organic forms using sunlight releases oxygen into the air, which will forever change the geography and biology of life on Earth. The Cyanobacteria also fix atmospheric nitrogen into organic forms. Their thylakoid stacks are visible within them.

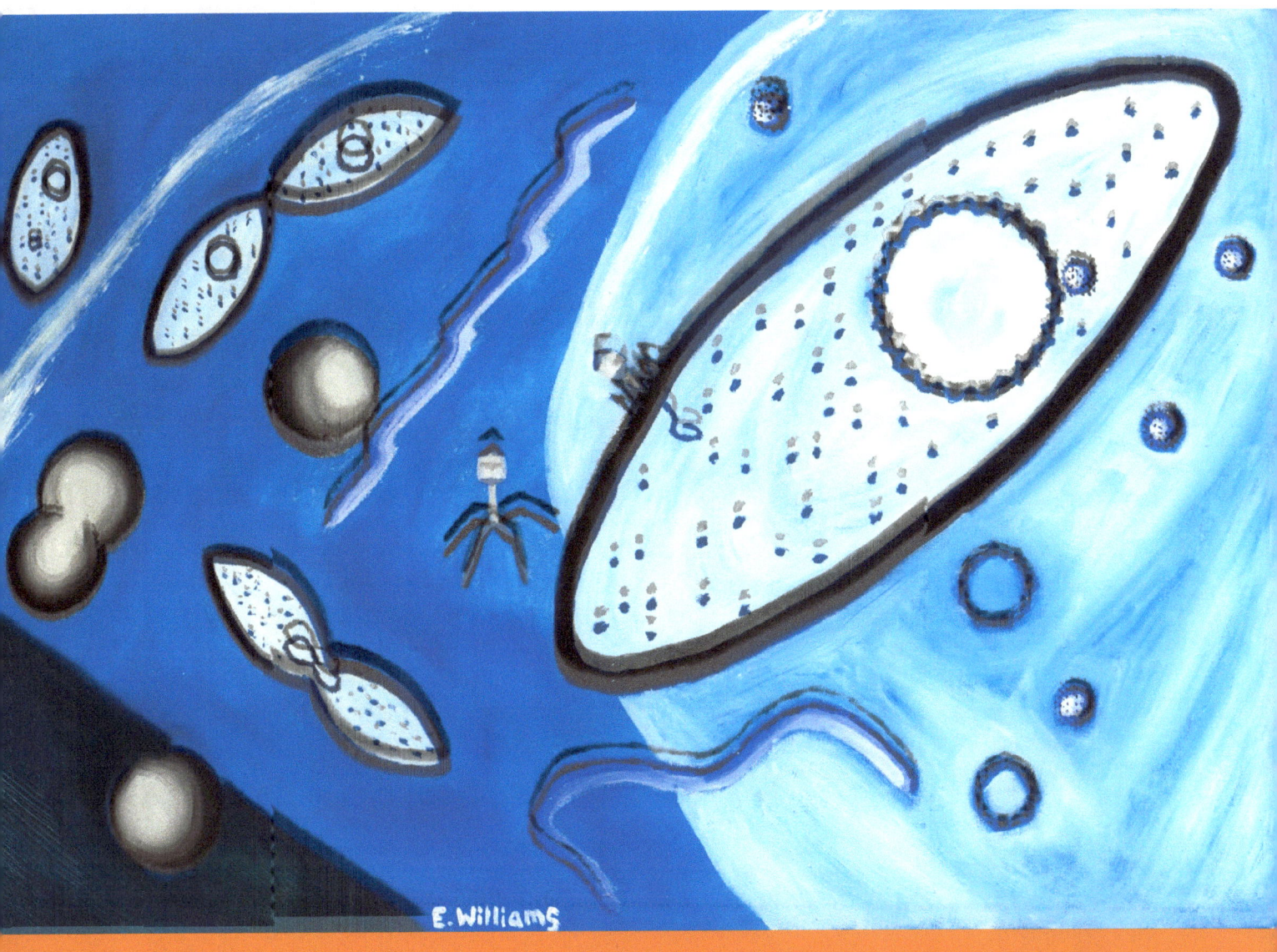

SWAZIAN PERIOD
MESOARCHEAN ERA 3500 M.Y.A.

"Monera"

The Kingdom Monera is born as the first membrane-contained bacteria evolve. DNA replaces RNA as the storage form of hereditary information in the bacteria, as it lacks a reactive oxygen group in its sugar backbone, making it more stable. RNA remains an intermediate transcribed molecule between DNA and protein. Bacteriophage viruses become wholly dependent on bacteria for their replication, and in turn infect them with extrachromosomal segments of circular DNA called plasmids. Prokaryotic bacteria, lacking a nucleus in their cells, will dominate Earth for the next 1.5 billion years – and even after this will far outnumber their Eukaryotic descendants. The bacteria rapidly undergo mitosis, beginning the chain reaction...

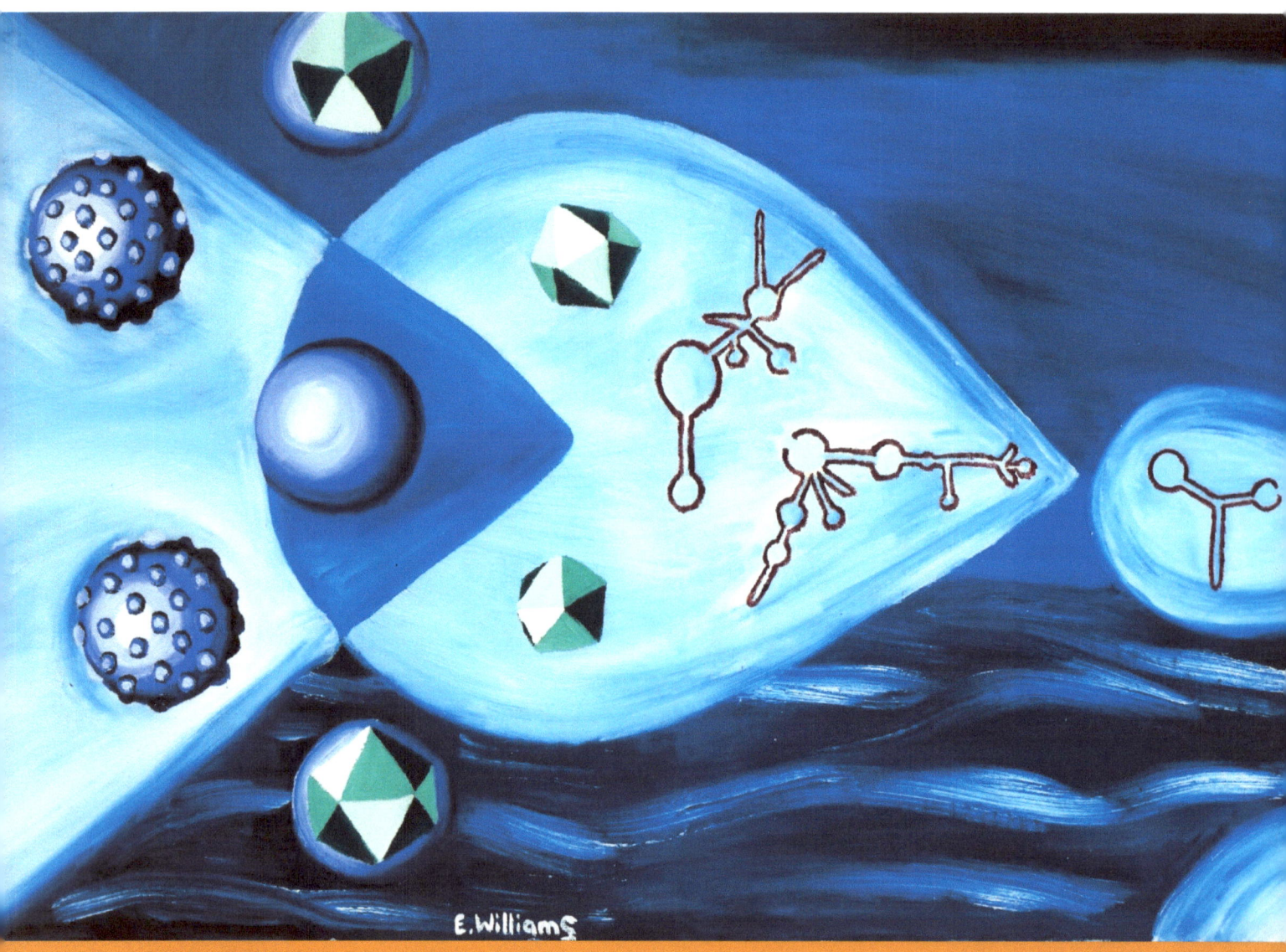

ISUAN PERIOD

3500 M.Y.A.
ARCHEAN EON

PALEOARCHEAN ERA

"RNA World"

Microdroplets of water show the complex structures of RNA, capable of acting as its own replication enzyme. The sequence of bases in RNA begins to be translated into the sequence of amino acids in proteins that serve to protect it, forming the first viral-like particles capable of self-replication.

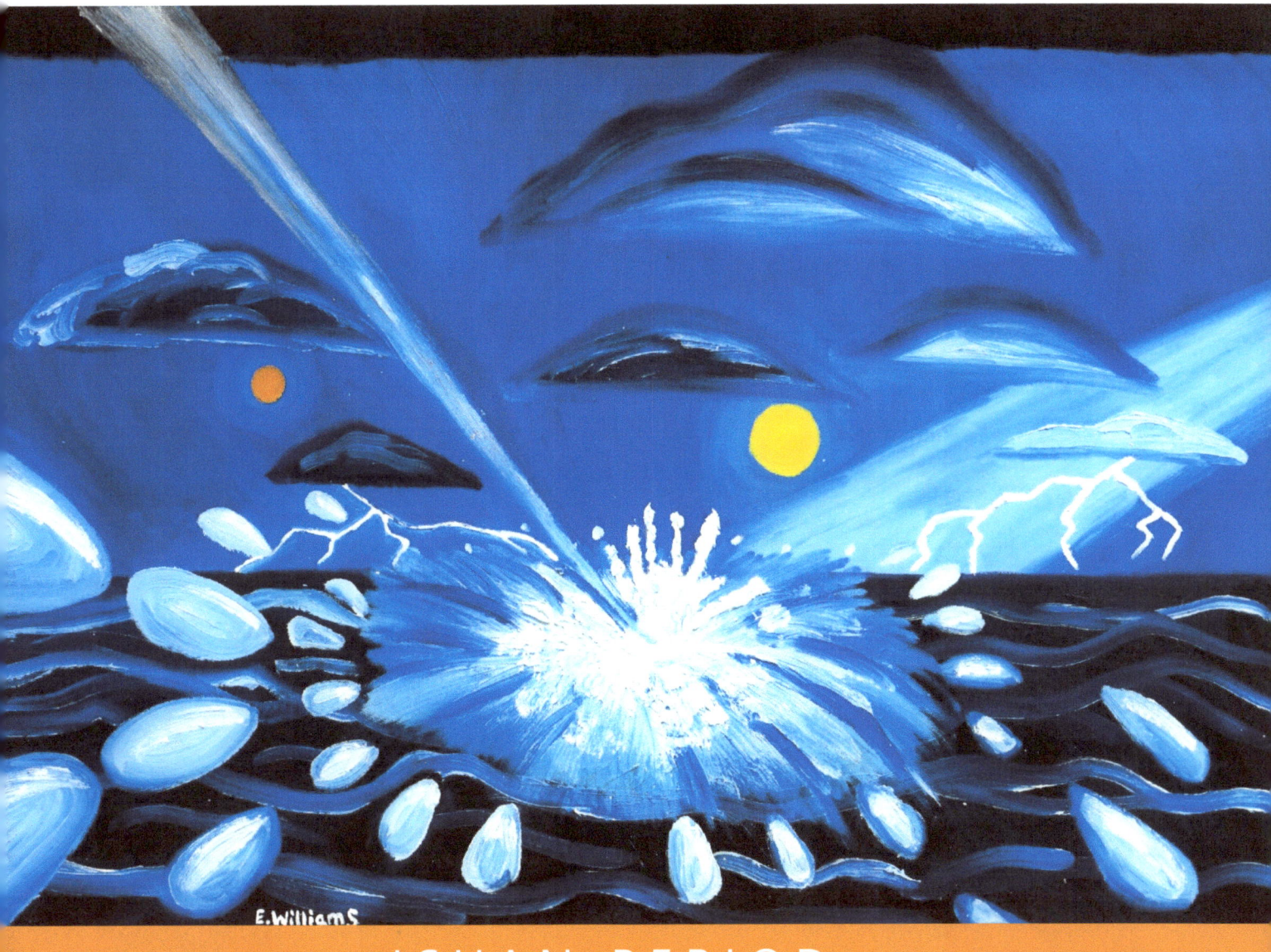

ISUAN PERIOD

PALEOARCHEAN ERA — 3800 M.Y.A.

"Inoculation"

Organic material is delivered to Earth by a comet, reacting with native organic compounds and an electric spark from lightning. Is this how the beginning of the chain reaction we call life begins? We will never know for certain. A jealous Venus looks on, already damned by runaway greenhouse gases to be forever devoid of life.

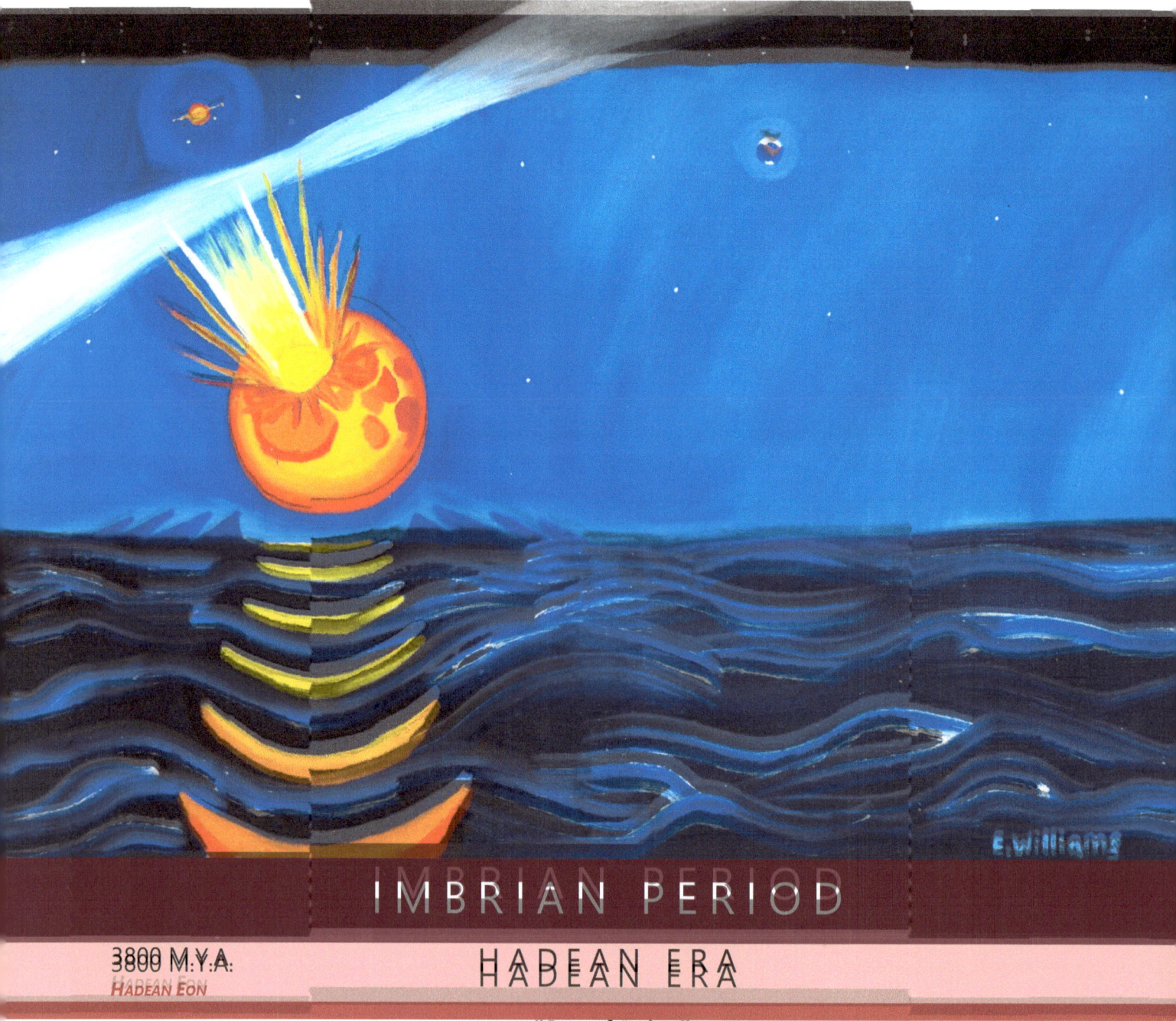

IMBRIAN PERIOD

3800 M.Y.A. HADEAN ERA

"Sea of Rains"

The impact giving rise to the Mare Imbrium, or Sea of Rains, occurs on the molten Moon and is visible from Earth. Tides are much more extreme due to the Moon's proximity. Jupiter with a visible ring looks on from the distance, as does an ocean-covered temperate Mars.

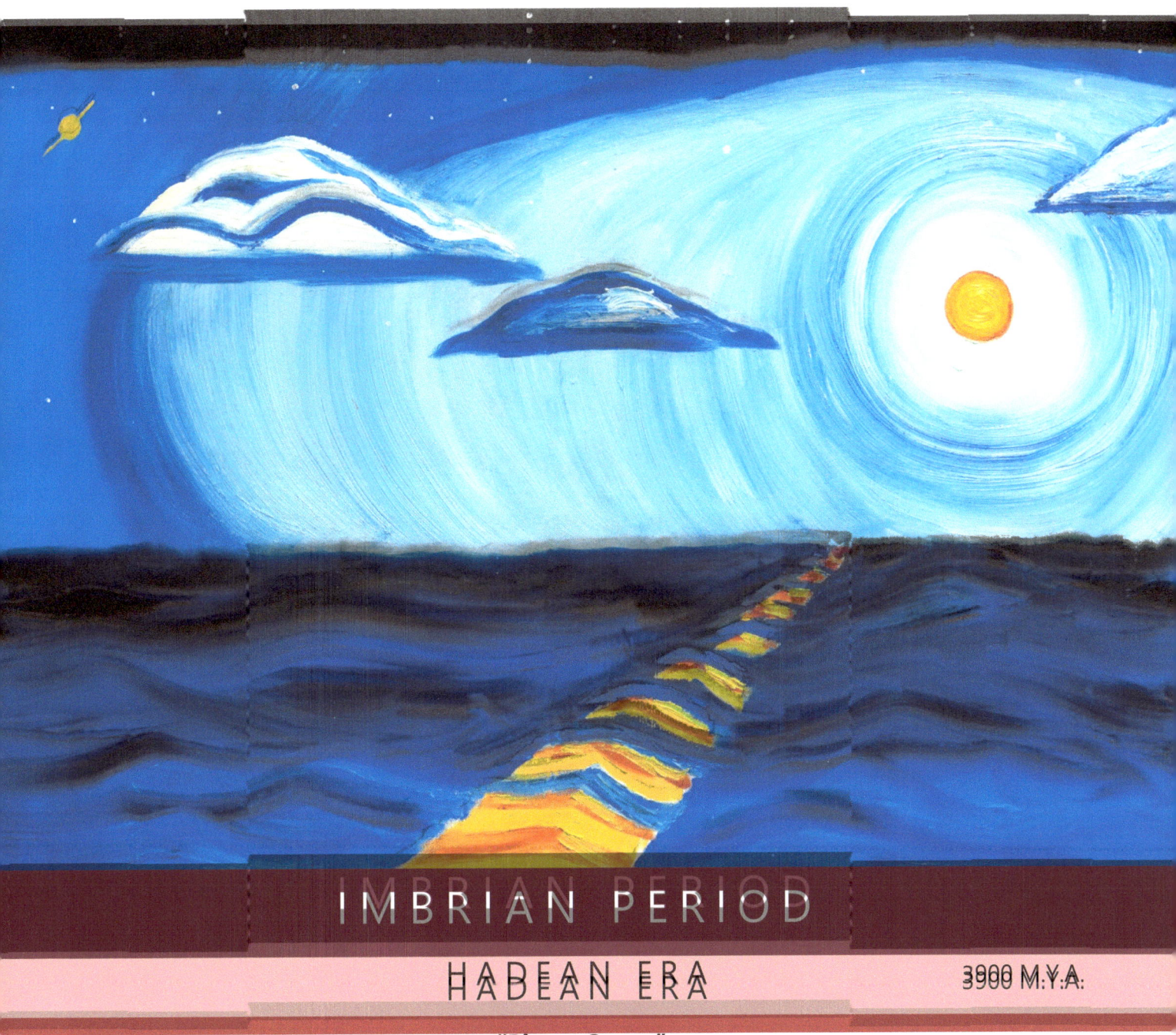

IMBRIAN PERIOD
HADEAN ERA — 3900 M.Y.A.

"Planet Ocean"

Saturn and the faint Sun look over the water-covered Earth. There is still no solid land.

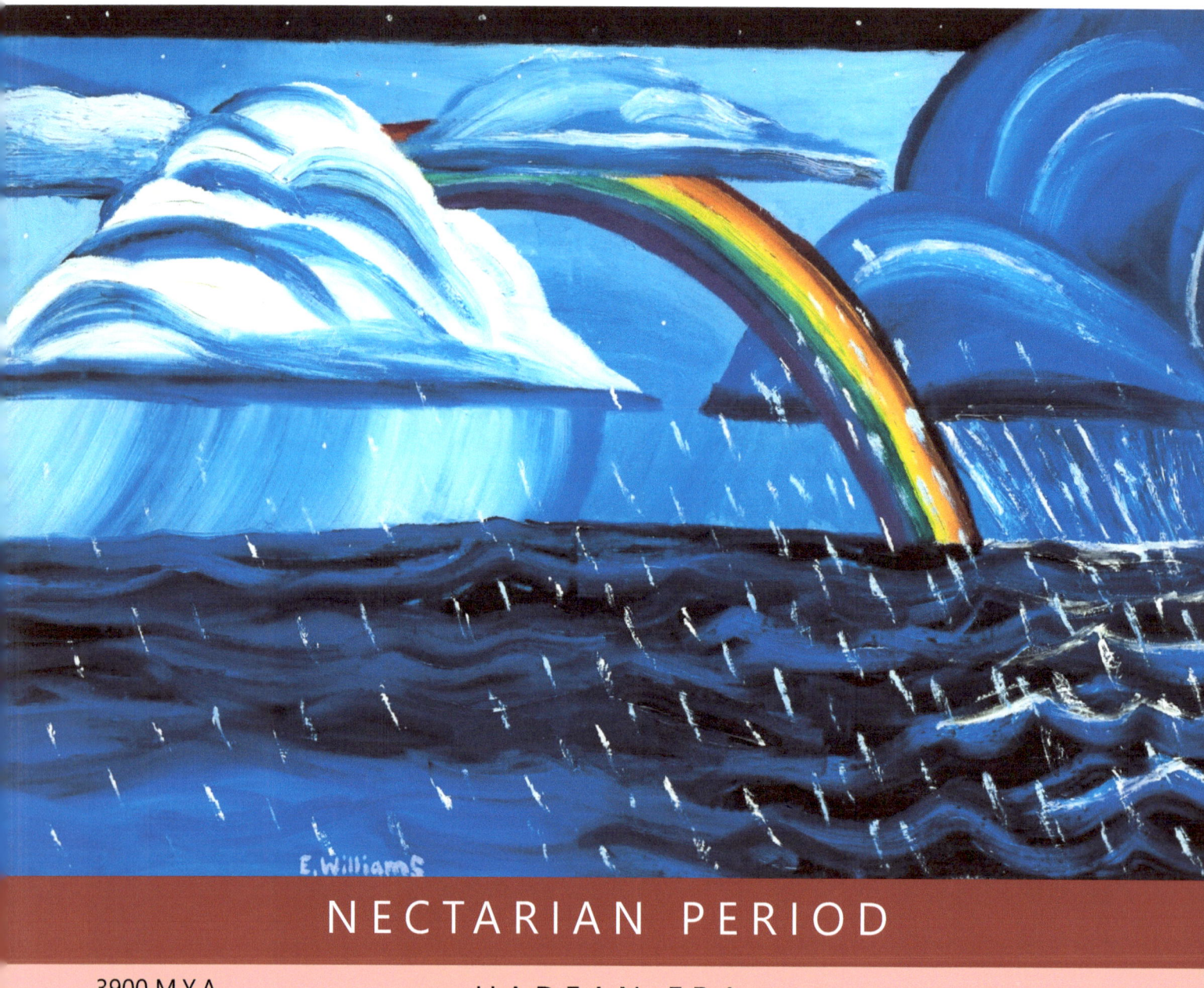

NECTARIAN PERIOD

3900 M.Y.A.
Hadean Eon

HADEAN ERA

"Waterworld"

A rainbow appears as the Earth becomes a little less violent. Rain continues to fall from the sky.

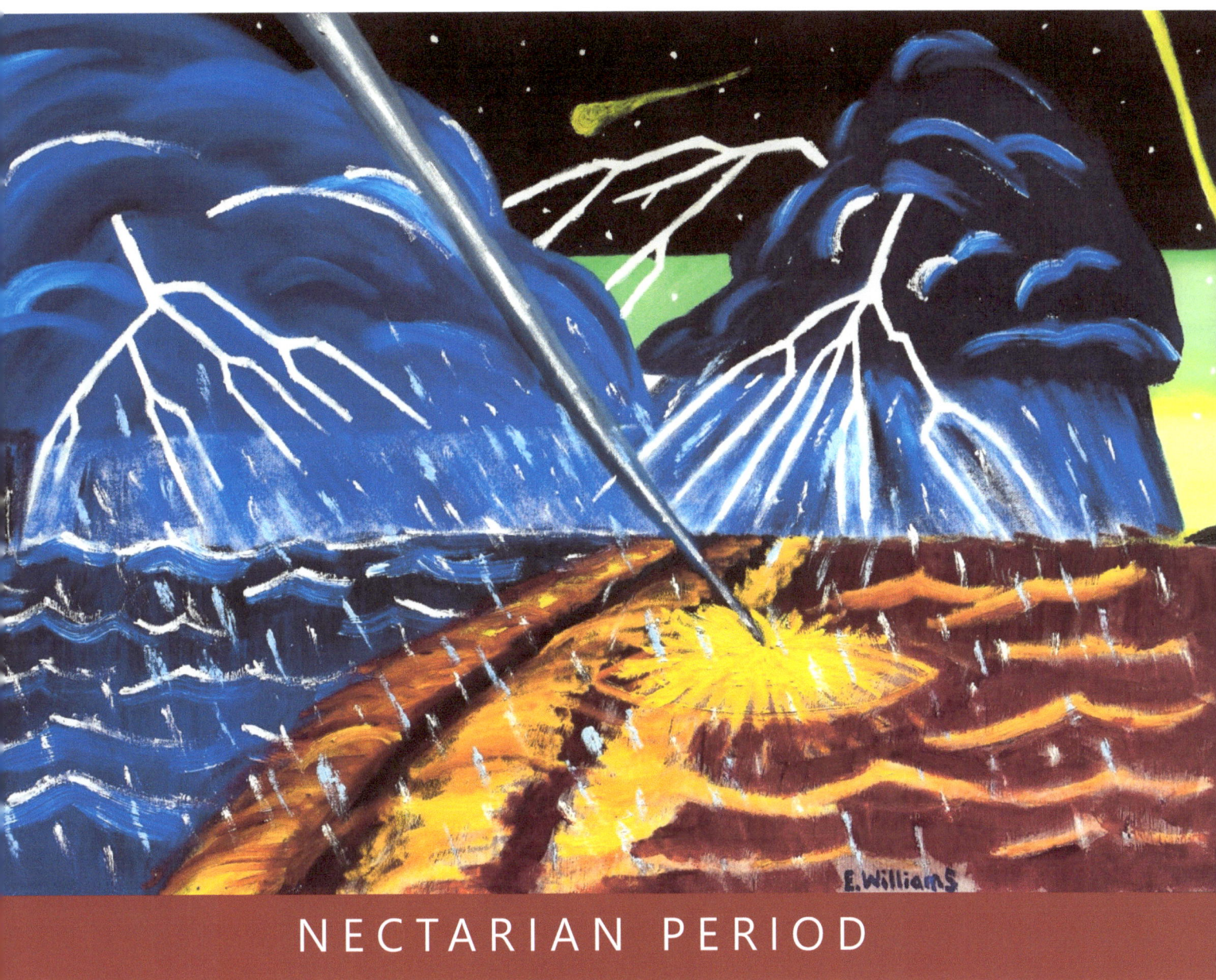

NECTARIAN PERIOD

HADEAN ERA

3975 M.Y.A.

"Flood"

Sufficient water delivered from comets and meteors, as well as from outgassing, allows rain to fall from Earth's thin atmosphere for the first time.

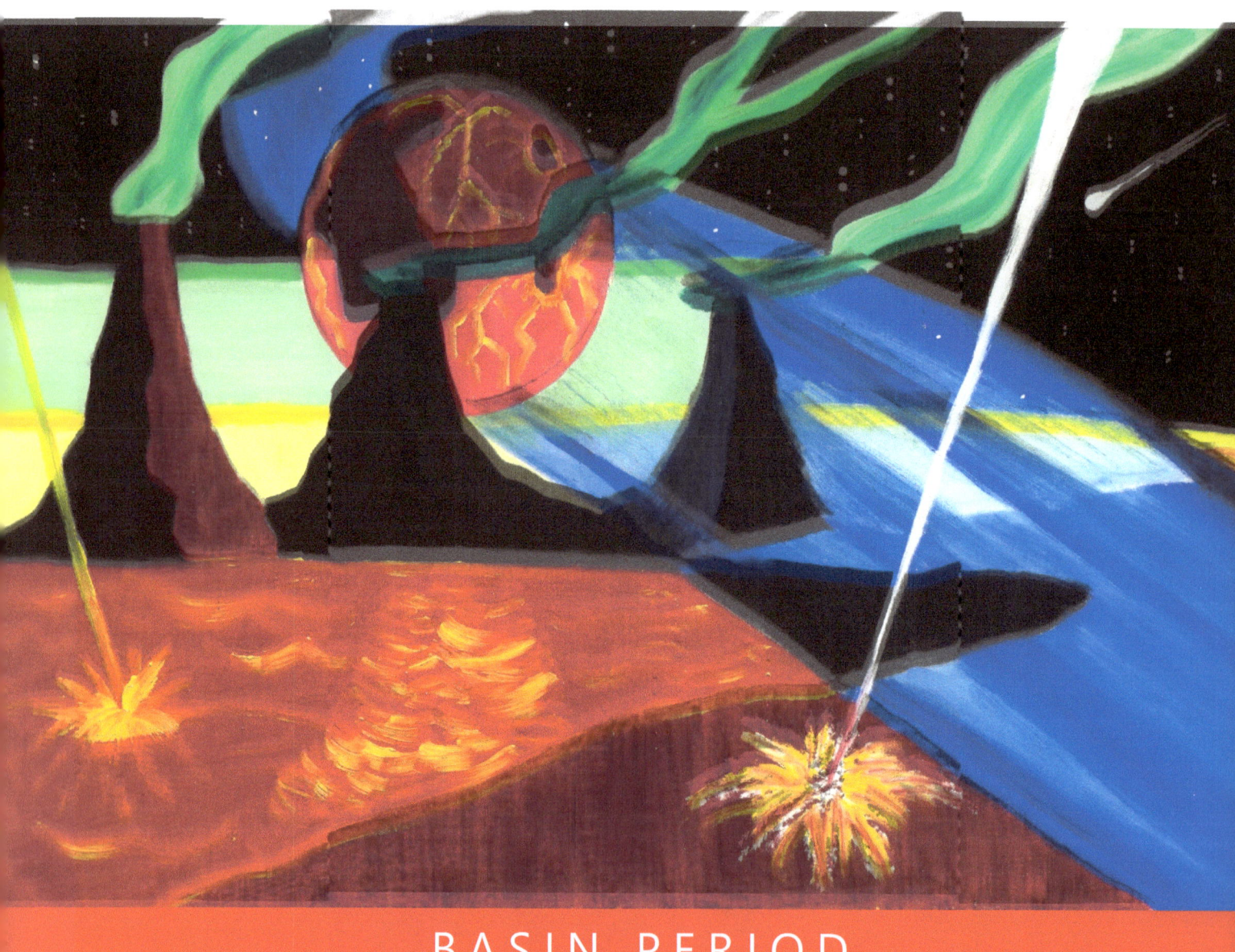

BASIN PERIOD

3975 M.Y.A. HADEAN ERA

HADEAN EON

"Full Moon"

The accretion of the Moon occurs from debris composed of Orpheus and Earth. The Moon is much closer to Earth than in the present time. Lava flows freely on both the Ocean Procellarum of the Moon and on Earth's molten surface.

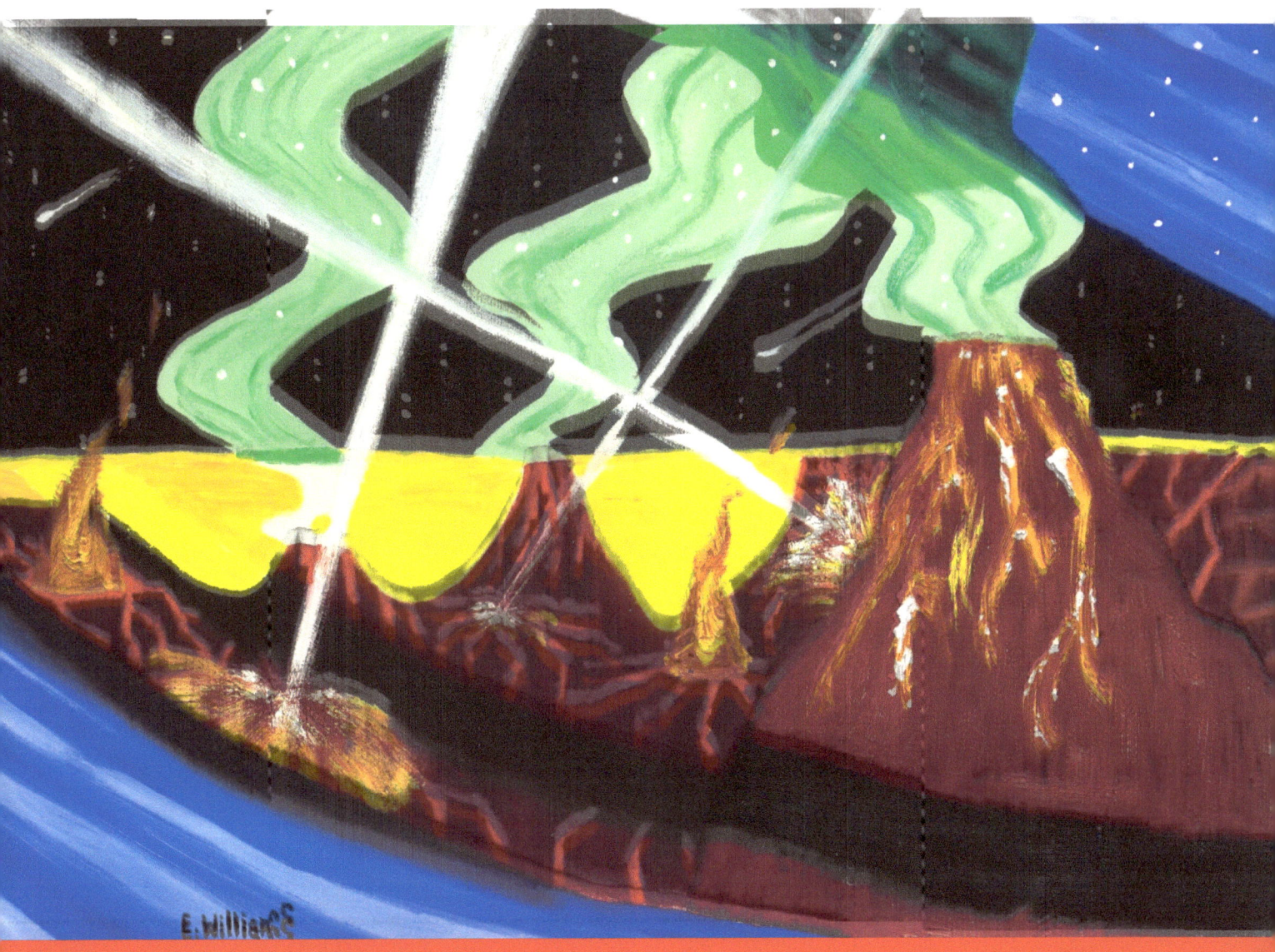

BASIN PERIOD

HADEAN ERA

4150 M.Y.A.

"Outgassing"

Gases from the Earth's interior are expelled into a thin atmosphere. Earth has a ring of ejecta from its collision with Orpheus.

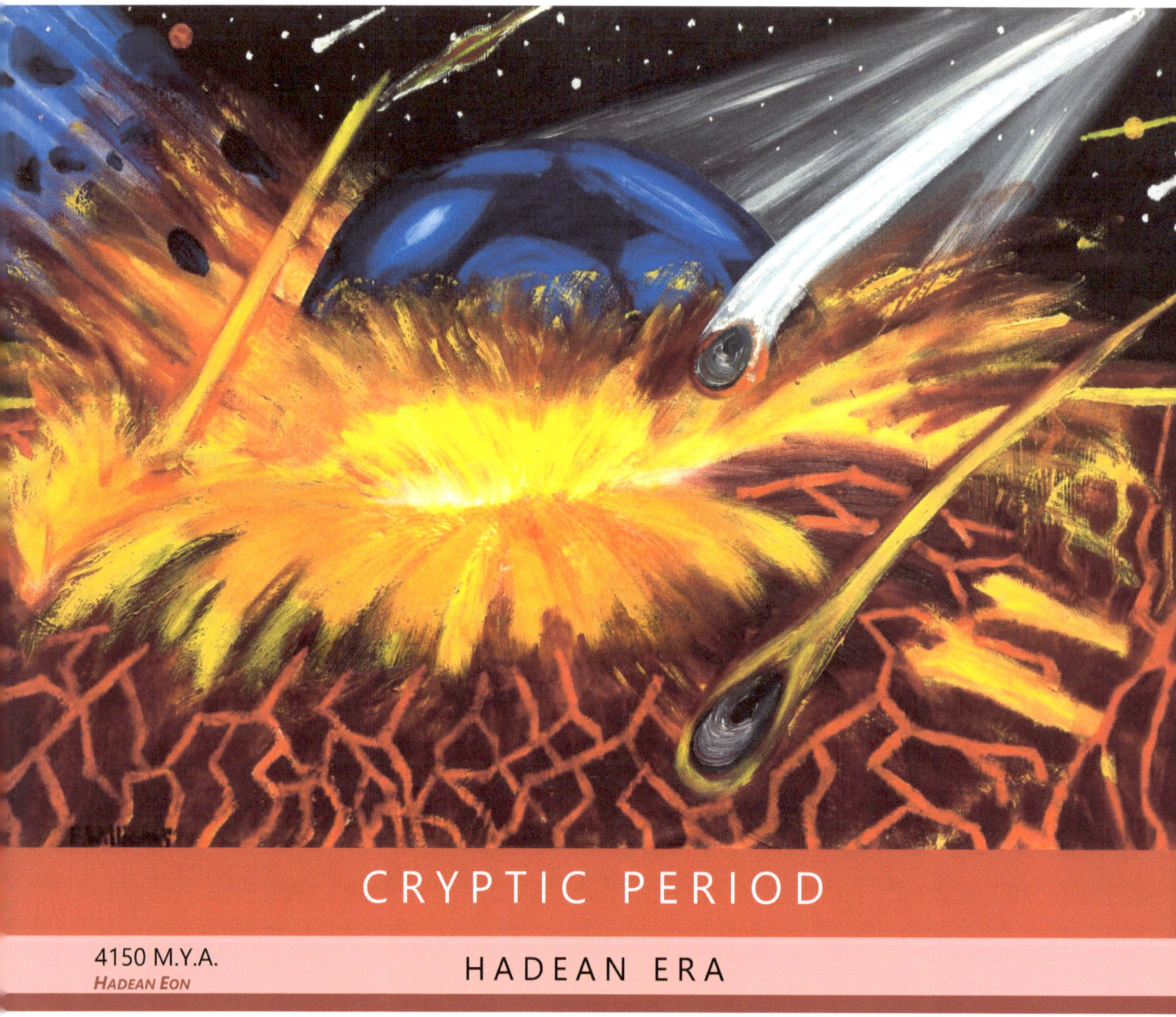

CRYPTIC PERIOD

4150 M.Y.A.
Hadean Eon

HADEAN ERA

"Orpheus"

The large proto-Moon Orpheus collides with the Earth, severely disrupting the crusts of both worlds, ejecting a mixture of both into orbit.

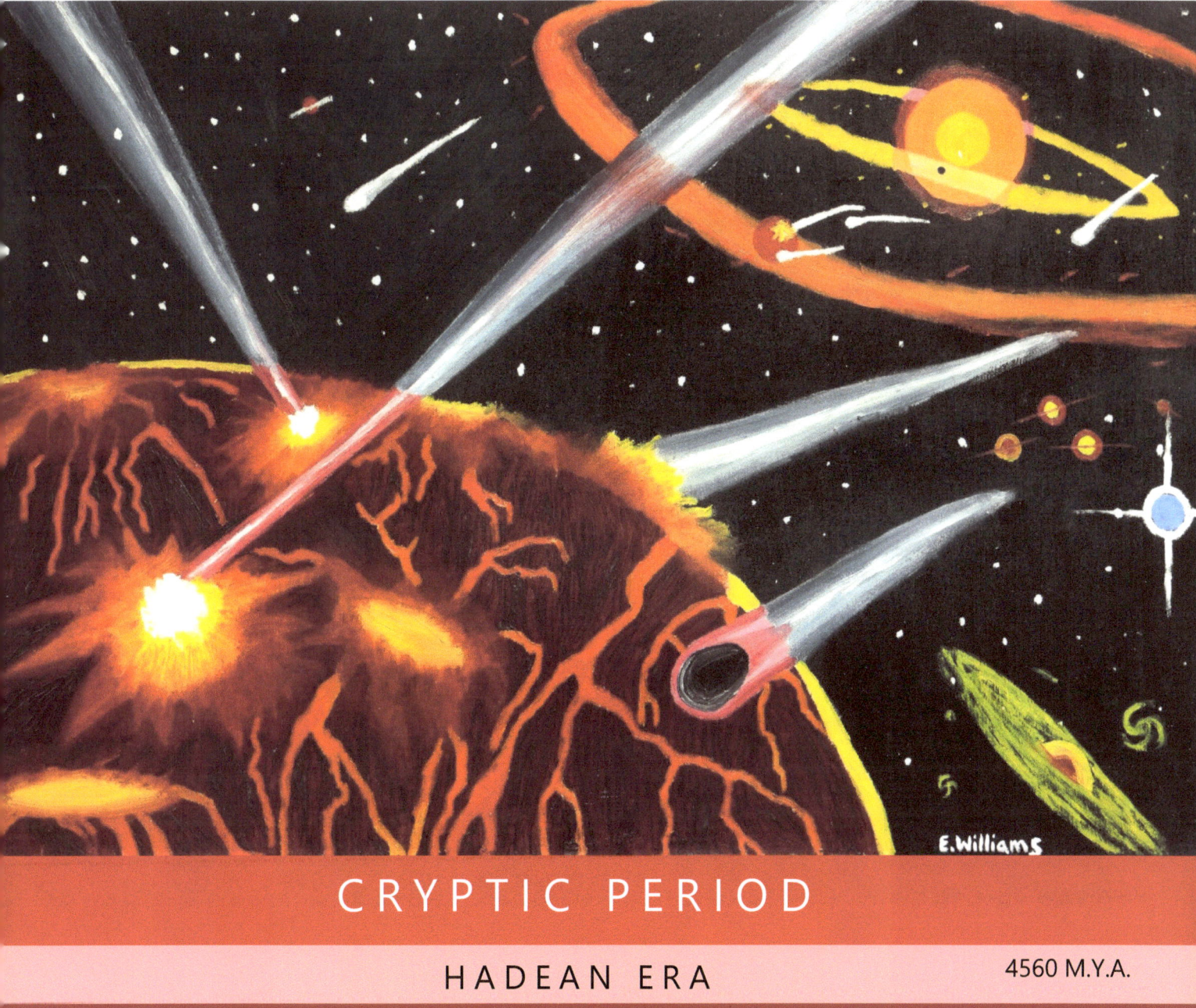

CRYPTIC PERIOD

HADEAN ERA — 4560 M.Y.A.

"Accretion"

The accretion of the Earth occurs in a series of violent collisions on its molten surface. The accretion of the inner planets Venus and Mercury is visible as rings around the faint young Sun.

A Chronicle of Earth in Deep Time
© 2018 Edward J. Williams and Patrick B. Williams

Note: the authors have taken aesthetic liberties with some factual components of Earth's history including the geographical distributions of animals and the naming of Earth's geological periods but have endeavored to remain as accurate as possible to current scientific understanding. Any and all factual errors are solely the fault of the authors.

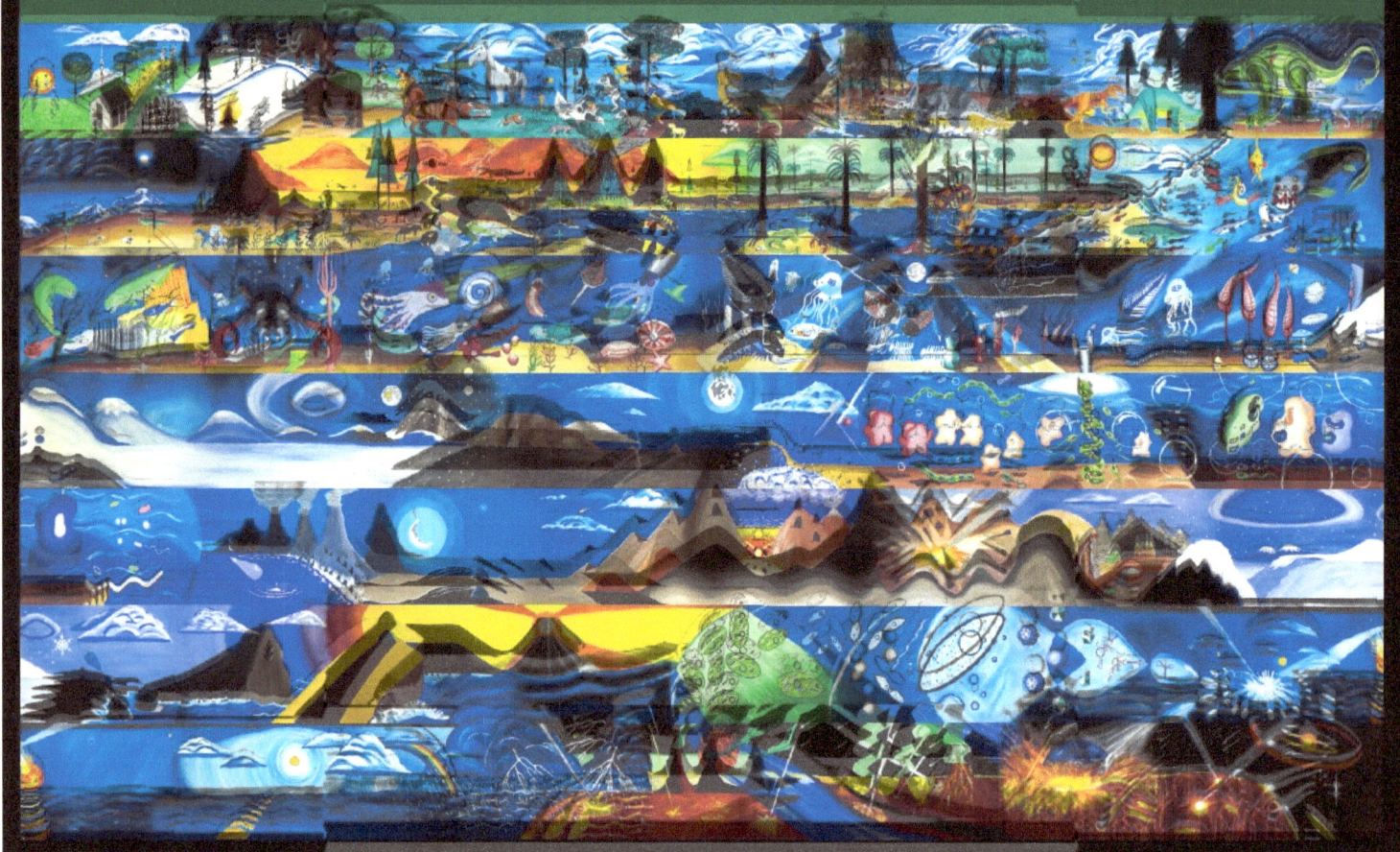

www.ingramcontent.com/pod-product-compliance
Lightning Source LLC
Chambersburg PA
CBHW051921210526
45473CB00006B/2090